M000190620

Dust of
Shooting Stars

by JEANETTE RICHARDSON HERRING

Copyright © 2020 by Jeanette Richardson Herring.
All rights reserved.

Published by Divine Ink Publishing, Anchorage, AK.

No part of this publication may be reproduced, distributed,
or transmitted in any form or by any means, including
photocopying, recording, or other electronic or mechanical
methods, without the prior written permission of the author
and publisher, except in the case of brief quotations embodied
in critical reviews and certain other noncommercial uses
permitted by United States of America copyright law.

For permissions requests, please contact the
author at Jeanette@PineMountainArts.com.

Front Cover Design: Valory Waligoski
Interior Layout Design: Standout Books

Contact the author via email at Jeanette@PineMountainArts.com
or through her website www.PineMountainArts.com.

Printed in the United States of America

ISBN (Print): 978-1-7341881-0-3
ISBN (eBook): 978-1-7341881-1-0

Dedicated to my darling, Chuck Herring.
You responded to my plea to know what love is.
You show me in countless unconditional ways
how to reach for the stars.

Table of Contents

Preface xi

As I am 1

The Tree of Life 7

One Point Many Views 8

The First Light 9

Poppies 10

Barricaded by Snow 11

I sit in the Balance 13

Dearest General Sherman .15

Slippery time 18

Fire. 19

We Exhale the Tree Inhales 21

Nature doesn't need people. 23

Ragged Raven 24

The Gray Fox 26

Winter Moon. 28

Blow Wind Blow 29

Waterfalling. 31

The Dust of Shooting Stars 33

A Little Story of Yayas – Sisters and Sisters-in-law 37

One Voice 38

Searching for the joy that only love can bring 39

Love all My Children. 42

In the Darkness of Night 46

Dreaming of Peace. 49

Daughter Mother Sister Wife. 51

The Circle of Grandmothers 52

Mother's letter on my 16th Birthday. 53

The Family Dinner 54

Sammie 57

What I still have — hope. 59

Love is an action Verb 61

The Tug of Family 63

Grandmother's Wisdom. 65

We're keeping June. 66

The Many Roles of the Other. 67

Meeting or Homecoming. 70

Circle of Friends. 72

Poetry and Photography with Friends. 73

Diving into the depths of love 73

Robbed of Hugs. 75

If You Know Me 78

We Have a Lilac Festival 80

Today. 82

The Gardener and the Garden 84

My Love for LIAV Camp 85

Girlfriends are the best. 86

In These Days. 88

The colors of love 89

Hopeful. 90

So Now They've Proven 92

True Love. 93

A poem of paradoxical proportions 95

How Often Do We Settle. 99

Does One Person Make a Difference 101

Caught Myself Judging Another. 102

May you know. 103

No word for love... 104

Kindness 106

Different Kinds of Happy 108

I Am Light. 112

Wind. Love. God. 113

In My Knower 115

Overcoming Darkness 117

Life is a Prayer 120

God Experiences 121

In the silence of the soul. 123

The Miraculous 125

Realization Floats. 128

Life Lessons 130

Who's God's Mommy 131

I've Been to the Center of the Sun 134

The Lost Word. 137

I Do not Pretend to Understand 139

Chameleon. 140

Life Lived on Social Media. 141

Up Praying for Truth 145

What cost kindness spoken 148

Moving forward from here 149

Soap in the Mouth. 150

The Light Leaking 156

Is This Love 157

Sometimes 159

Vision or Dream? 160

Freedom in Letting Go. 162

I have to be ready to let go 164

So They Say No 165

My Time is My Own? 168

The Path to Truth 171

Pure LOVE 172

Perfection. 173

Saying Yes 174

Keepin' the lights a Burnin' 177

Layers. 179

Some Thoughts on Thinking and Truth. 180

Every heart has a story 182

Full of funerals. 185

The Living Tombstone 186

Facing Death 187

She Wrote her Death in her Life. 189

No Names to Mark the Days 191

Never the Same 192

32 seconds – 9 dead 195

Have I Expired? 197

Sunday thinking on a Saturday .198

When Silence is Cruel 203

Hard to see in the chill of loss 204

The Caged Heart 205

Tick Tock 207

As the sun rises 209

Scent matters 210
Retired Rewired Reworked 211
Google what? 213
I may be done. 214
The years I cried in silence 219
There's Light in Me Yet 223
Words 226
Write Write Write 227
Aha moments 229
Culinary Arts 230
Creative Inspiration 231
Love for the Arts 232
In a Paradise Lost. 234
Words fall from the sky 236
Poetically thinking. 238
And this is me 240
The Irish Experience. 241
Testing my Muse 242
Metaphorically speaking 244
No Black or White. 245
Coffee with Mary. 246
Dear Agatha 247
Birthing Poetry 249
In Honor of an Artist Friend 250
Revelation 251
Haiku Times 2. 253
Worth Knowing. 254
In the Heart of the Poet 255

Acknowledgements 256
Special Acknowledgement for Poetry with Friends 258
About the Author 259
Image Credits 260

"Tears are words that need to be written."
— Paulo Coelho

Preface

I lay on the sun-warmed sidewalk staring up into the night sky, asking the stars: "Why am I here?" I was seven years old. Ever curious and seeking answers, my childhood was riddled with questions. Neighbor ladies took turns taking me to churches telling me if I tarried long enough, said the right prayers, and was dunked in water, I'd have my answers. I'd be saved. Saved? I was hoping I'd be saved from my father's mean-spirited words and behavior. I was a little girl; I didn't know his anger wasn't my fault or what alcoholism was. That didn't happen. At least not how I imagined.

The difficulties I experienced in childhood led me to find ways to find real sanctuary in nature, music, art, and books. I read voraciously, expanding my world with wondrous fictional adventure and mystery. I discovered journaling was a safe place to reveal my hurt and to continue to seek answers. Along the way, I expanded my world of words—they became the palette that later colored my writing, teaching, and how I learned.

I've worked, married, mothered, and divorced. I thought I'd found my life partner. Together, we battled cancer for six years, until he lost his battle. When his breath vanished so did my identity as wife, caretaker, mother. I was heartbroken. Needing to find renewed meaning, I sought answers anywhere I thought they might be waiting: Work. Family. Structures from my past. An insatiable desire to learn. Multifaceted career opportunities. Visiting world cultures, innumerous joys and sorrows. No one thing felt like the path I was seeking.

Nine years ago, still staring at the stars wondering, I decided to walk away from my life as an arts administrator. I re-wired. I continued to use my imagination, create art, and write. Starting a new lifestyle meant down-sizing memories and "stuff." A surprise changed the course of my life—Mom had kept all my boxes of writings and a full house of stuff. As I de-cluttered, I found my heart expanded with room for more love. The "used ta' be tour" that was backward looking was traded for increased listening, creating, and writing new works. I'm basking in the daily moments, discovering, uncovering and recovering—me. I found the path I had been searching for all those years.

Serendipity may have led you to this moment. Perhaps, you've been looking at the stars for answers to life's questions, hoping some star dust of revelation and hope would fall from the skies. You may think that what you're holding in your hand is just another book. My strong desire is that it acts like a mirror—when you look into it you see parts of yourself. The sanctuary that comforted me in childhood is now, more than I could have imagined, an essential part of the road I currently travel. These poems represent the journey of understanding; the way ahead that I walk and my view toward the stars are tied: that which is before me and that which shines above me.

What I'm sure of is that we are all more alike than different. And there is comfort and hope in that belief. We are all star dust after all.

"Fill your paper with the breathings of your heart."
— William Wordsworth

I'd love to hear from you. I believe every heart has a story to tell. Please, feel free to share yours with me. Jeanette@ PineMountainArts.com

As I am

I've been writing since I was 25. Yes, I've seen growth, maturity and relapses in the years. I shared my feelings, understandings and the serious issues that worried me. I cried over injustices and unfairness in lives of those I loved and those I didn't even know. I've read of my innocence, and ignorance. I laughed and considered my weight, age, abilities, and progress. What I learned and studied was sprinkled throughout the pages. Journals of questions, prayers, poems, hopes and dreams, stories from my heart, mixed with lists of arts advocacy plans to build retreats and galleries. It's safe to say not many things escaped my pen.

I read my writings
To know who
or what I want
By reading
My
Life
In words
I see my history
View my story
Feel my tears
Re-live my fears
Through the years
I wrote
Made plans

I wrote of pain and sorrow
I wrote of not knowing
Who I was if I was
No longer
Wife
   Husband died
Mother
   Children grown
Arts administrator
   Walked away
These titles were
What I did
That gave my life meaning
I wifed
Took care
Cooked beautiful meals
Decorated
Entertained
Cleaned
Tried to understand
Loved Loved Loved
I mothered
Mine and his
Comforted
Cared
Taught
Shared
Guided
Made mistakes

Lots of mistakes
Loved Loved Loved
Career worker, supporter
Wage earner, encourager
My identity wrapped
In these three titles
Try again wifed again
Divorced
Mother to my own and theirs
All grown gone
I read of the angst
My concern
Did I let God down
Did I disappoint
Will
I ever know love
Or who I am if
I'm no longer how
I identified myself
Now I read those
Words
I hug that woman
I forgive her
I have compassion
For the one that was
Me
Accepted
Friended

Loved
It's OK to have been
All those feelings and
Identities and losses
Understanding sweeps
Clean the slate
I recognize her in her pain
If I'm not all these
Then who am I
Searching for truth
Realization of doing
Is not being
Trying so hard to please
Succeed
Heal
Be loved for who you were
But even you didn't know
Who that was
You were too busy doing
Wife
Mother
Career woman
Survivor
Working at being the best
Worrying that you'd failed
Trying to make things right
That probably didn't
Need doing at all

Placing all your value
On your doing
Never on just rejoicing
In your creative being
The unique being
That you are
Now looking back
From a different
Perspective I hardly recognize
This woman
Now I say thank you
You got us through
To being who we are today
I'm finally content
As I am

The Tree of Life

Stretching upwards to the light
Digging downwards into the earth
Providing shelter and sustenance
The tree of life grows

The heart of the redwood
Flexibility and forgiveness of the willow
Fragrance of the pine to heal
The tree of life nurtures

Taking in the poisonous air
Breathing out life into our souls
Providing shade from the heat
Sacrificing self for fire to warm us
The tree of life provides

Sighing in the wind
Come be with me
Rejected, maimed and harmed,
Forming scars over wounds
The tree of life survives

Decorated with baubles and lights
Trimmed, shaped and tamed
Forgotten tossed aside
Chewed up, turned to mulch
The tree of life begins anew

One Point Many Views

Looking out towards the mountains
From the same spot on the deck
The view changes every few minutes
Not always spectacular monumental changes
More like whisper cloud movements
Breeze blowing leaves
Birds flying and calling
Shadows glance against the rocks
Shimmering web
Like life the view is not stagnant

The First Light

The first light
Upon the mountain crest
Comes in like a wave
At low tide
Seeping over the ridge
It rises slowly
Lazily
Taking its time to
Splash color into the darkness
Revealing beautiful surprises
Right in front of us

Poppies

The joy of the first bloom
Spring poppies
My eye wanders
Over the hillside awaiting
Hints of orange
Will it be a good
Poppy year
Add lupine
Lilac
Colors
A profusion of happiness
On a green stem
There
Look
There
Here they come
Out of the dusty beige
The rocks come alive
Their heads turned
To Mecca
Their beauty unfolds
Standing tall
In the sun
Sleeping
With the moon
Oh yes when the poppies come
Life returns from the gray gloom

Barricaded by Snow

Forced retreat
Snow encased
Letting go
Of the let goes
Barricaded by cold
Icy berms
Squirrels creating avalanches
The trees are snowing
Chance taking
Not worth the making
When home is warm
Enjoying deploying
Snow shovel by shovel
Wheel barrel full
Until back aches
It'll be there tomorrow
Hot cocoa
Cookies
Suffice
From the Christmas
That didn't happen
Or did it
in the beauty of silence
Perhaps it came
Covering us over
To be still

Celebration only postponed
No reason to
Escape this cocoon
Our wings are tucked tightly
Not ready to fly
Maybe later
I hear there's a new year
Coming

I sit in the Balance

Full Moon is setting
Sun is rising into the darkness
While I sit in the balance
For my heart is seeking
Answers to questions
Not yet queried
This isn't surprising
It's more often
I "suppose" the answers
Before I've asked
Keeping the question at bay
It isn't real until it's named
Crippled by indecision of what to say
For fear of forming it into words
Knowing all words spoken can
Give life to what they name
Yet my heart knows what I seek
And until I ask there will be no answers
Trust says ask away
For the answers are given
When you know what to request
Time is now as the sun rises
And the moon sets

GENERAL SHERMAN

Dearest General Sherman

(Largest, most empathetic tree in the world)

As I wandered through the redwood grove your magnificent presence captured my entire being. You stopped me and my breath simultaneously to view your grand visage and sense your powerful connection to earth and heaven. My tears of loss were met by your sighs as the wind gently caressed your branches. I was awestruck with your stateliness and the beating of your heart in tune with the universe. As we sat together you taught me the lessons of centuries of life filled with torture and pain, and how scarred over wounds gave you strength for the next storm. We talked of the life growing within you and being nurtured and protected by your deep roots and uplifting nature. As you impressed upon my mind that it is all eternal, the continuous reaching for the heavens and digging in deep for your own sustenance. The sharing of breath as you take in our poisonous air and return it cleansed and oxygenated. You silently healed my soul with your wisdom of the ages and the lessons you so lovingly shared with me. You taught me that love never ends. To say I love you is incomplete, not nearly enough. You comforted me, you granted me room in your heart and held me fast as I wept for the one being carried away wrapped in evergreen angel wings.

I am One with the Tree

Be the tree, be the love
See the redwood from the roots to above
See the nurturing from the earth

Plant your feet, look with eyes that naturally do not see
To see what is visible only through Me

I saw the energy rising up as golden shafts of light from below
I saw the light from above, golden still
I know the heart of the redwood beats with mine.
Breath pulled in sharply with the beauty,
Breath escaped with a sigh,
How is it I
Am allowed to see this mystery of life

Be still, do not move, no distractions
Be still, pay attention, pay attention
I am deeply calm
My heart and hands turned upward
Heat rising from my palms
Turning inward to my heart
How to explain, where do I start
I see angel wings around my friend
There is peace that will not end
Stop thinking, and simply see
This is life, life with Me
See the tree, see your heart
They are growing and not apart
You are one with all
Expanding as the tree
You are all one
with Me no fear
No goodbyes

Just farewells and deeply felt sighs
It's for me I cry, I say to the tree
I cry with you, says the one called Me.
I am in the tree, the smile, the tears
I am with you throughout the years
For eternity is where I am,
Look deep where love resides
I placed my hand upon the hand
I knew was on my shoulder
Holding it tenderly,
I sank down upon the boulder
Overcome with the love that came with each breath
Once again reminded, without doubt, there is no death

Slippery time

Time is slippery
Grasping
It slides away
Running in rivulets
Escaping and taking
Loved ones with it
Mudslides
Torrential downpour
Reaching for a branch
Anything to slow the descent
Popping up to breathe
A nanosecond of consciousness
A moment of cognizant
Thinking
Slapped away by the returning
Recycling winds
Back in the rapidly running
Flow
Hurricane forces
Into the vortex hold your breath
Here we go again

Fire

Fire comes
Consuming everything
Cathedral
Forest
Home
Good
Bad
Fire knows no difference
It burns
It brings light to the darkness
It turns beauty into rubble
The water comes
Quenches the pain
Soothes the burns
Washes the gaping holes
Reveals life
Brings hope
It knows no boundaries
It flows over good
Or covers over bad
Life begins in water
Death is revealed by fire
Yet
Seeds pop from fire's heat
We water our seeded
Prayers in tears

Angels
Nature
Humanity
Respond to fire's
Devastation
We will build, plant, restore
Cathedral
Forest
Home

We Exhale the Tree Inhales

Life is so rich and complex
Moment by moment in flux
We exhale
The tree inhales
The breath of the interchange
Is experienced by another
As an exchange
A whisper of breath
Upon the cheek
No choice is just our own
We move and the ripples
Flow outward as in a pond
We extend love or anger
Fear or joy
The world around us responds
Another feels the emotional pull
Caught up in the energy
We can feel the warmth
Or chill of the heart
We seek not just for answers
We look for the process
Of knowing
Understanding
Growing
Deepening our existence
Connection

To the known and unknown
Diving deeper
Into ourselves
We bring others with us
Into the well
What will we find together
For we really do all things
Together
Inhale
Exhale
From the moment we are born
Until we die
We are a part of the whole
Perhaps even after
Our influence will still be felt
As a wave upon the seas

Nature doesn't need people

People need nature
Harrison Ford
States the obvious
But unspoken
Truths of life
On planet earth
Global warming
Trash and litter
Fracking and mining
Burning or slashing
forests and glades
For instant gratification
Greed and power
Impacts us and our
Future generations
The planet continues
Denuded or covered
In water – even sludge
Our life and future lives
Are the ones that will
Change and probably
Not for the good
For all that call
Our beautiful planet
Home.

Ragged Raven

Flying by jagged
his wings 'tis sure
One is ragged
the other pure

No lopsided flying
No what's wrong with me sighing
Scavenging his darling's breakfast
While she sits calmly in the nest

No excuses he offers
A morsel does he proffer
Seeking his darling's pleasure

Not losing sight of his treasure

Bringing life from death
Recycling at best
He returns from his flight
To the one of all the others
The only one for whom he'd fight

He became ragged
In her defense
Protecting the nest
She sees his wounds
As feathered proof
As he proudly flies
One wing ragged
The other true

The Gray Fox

Layers
Of snow
Tracked by the
Gray fox
Marked a straight path
Not my way
I'm a series of stops
Filled with curiosity
Turn right
Left
A round mandala
Infinity style
Mind wanders
Heart leaps
Splits in many directions
Changes again
To be a gray fox
In a straight line
To the destination
One foot fall
Mirroring the next
Intentional
Directional
Functional
Could be — but
Not my way

Mysterious
Surprise me with joy
Challenge the path
What's next
Jump over the log
Falling
Rolling
Now that's my way

Winter Moon

The winter moon of morning
Reflects the light of the unseen sun
Misty earth reaches to heaven
Inviting us to join in the awakening

Blow Wind Blow

Come my mistral Muse
Bring insight and understanding
Rustling words among the leaves
Inspiration fly upon the wing
Breathe love and life into me

Blow
Wind
Blow
Take away everything
   I think
      I know
Clear the path of obstacles and debris
Allow the past to be swept free of me

In this
     Moment
     Pause

Listen for whispers in the breeze
Silence
Stillness
Serenity
Free of condemnation
Determination
To hear creation
Let go the desire to conclude

What's yet to come
Let the wind
Cleanse my soul

Blow
Wind
Blow
Twisting gusts of truth and beauty
Clicking heels of slippers ruby
In finding home
Discovering I never left
Revealing the truth of Oz
Courage • Heart • Brain
Was always here
Upon the wind

Waterfalling

While sitting quietly
Next to the roar
Of the water falling
Splashing off rocks
Gurgling around stones
Whirling its way
Through tree stumps
Determined to reach
The valley floor
I'm in awe of the ability
Of a tiny molecule
Becoming a drop
Forming a puddle
Meeting a creek
Gathering together
Building momentum
Aimed at one destination
Allowing gravity with no effort
To create such majestic
Beauty and power
Flowing freely
Creating
Journeying
Arriving
Dispersing
Nourishing nature
Quenching thirst
From such a tiny start

The Dust of Shooting Stars

My skin is holding
a whole universe
filled with the dust
of shooting stars
and galaxies
just waiting to be set free
pulsating
pushing
prodding
to rejoin the source of life
Banging into false notions
Stripping away the hardened
shell of opinion
Judgment of self and others
Resentment
Blame
Fear
Dishonesty
To reveal the
Light
Love
Energy of eternity
Residing within the thin veneer of self
Death is not required to escape
To blazon this truth
And shine in this moment

To be fully star light
Brighten the darkness
Yes.
Me. You. Us.

Diving Into The
Depths of
Love

A Little Story of Yayas – Sisters and Sisters-in-law

My mom and her sisters by marriage are the yayas. Last time we were in Hawaii together Mom and Aunt Evie (my father's baby sis) went wandering down to the water's edge hand in hand whispering and giggling steadying each other in the sand, oblivious to anyone else on the beach – caught up in their 70 years of memories and each other. I watched in awe from the patio. A few years later, my sister friend Jan and I did the same on a California beach. We giggled and held hands and talked of hopes and dreams and of course her love for her husband and family and how she hoped their lives would be well and happy once she was gone. She wanted that for me too. Never one to tell me what to do – I knew she wanted more for me than my life then held. I was miserable in a bad marriage and Jan had pancreatic cancer and we love/loved each other. We were the next generation of soulmate yaya sisters. Jan left us just a few months later. I divorced shortly after. The realization that life is too special to waste worrying over sickness or repeatedly trying to fix a bad marriage. Enjoying and savoring every moment of life matters. I risked the unimaginable and stepped out to find love. When Mom met my new sweetheart she told me he was my mirror and she was exceedingly happy for me. A year later Mom was surrounded by our love as she too passed. As I sit here now embraced by Chuck's love, I know they are smiling and cheering me on. Now Aunt Evie and I walk the beach hand in hand remembering all the yayas while we whisper and giggle holding hands steadying each other in the sand.

One Voice

May my very be-ing
Orchestrate joy and love
Create a symphony of freedom
Notes climbing scales
Children keeping
The pastorale melody
Dancing
Energizing
Connecting
To the harmony of the universe
All becoming one
Voice
Rhapsody
Melody
Sweet song of life

Searching for the joy that only love can bring – is an inside job.

One Saturday at a BBQ I met a lady that was so delightfully open with me. She was sharing with me about her experiences with online dating on an over 55 dating site. I just listened as she said: "You are too young for this singles site, or maybe to understand this but, when people get my age… (I laughed to myself that she didn't think I was yet 55) then quickly paid closer attention as she went on – "We've lived long enough to know what we want and we expect that the other person also knows what they want – that it is useless to take up the time of someone who isn't exactly what you are looking for." We don't have the time to waste – life is going by so fast " I commented: "If this is so, then there is no sense of rejection. Because, it doesn't make either wrong, just not right for you." She responded: "Yes! The key for me was to learn to love myself as much as I love and adore my grandchildren." She stopped, smiled and went on – "I want only the best for them, I have now learned that is what I needed to want for me too. I am having the best year of my life meeting new people and knowing who and what I want is OK and that I can have just that – it is liberating." She turns a very active 70 next month.

I came away from the BBQ with yet another beautiful new insight. Online dating, jobs, pastimes, everything I do and everyone I spend time with is being given a gift of my time and me, theirs. Do I have the time to waste doing things that aren't really what I want? Do I love myself as much as I do my kids, grandkids, favorite friends or critter? *Asking myself would I want this life experience for my loved one? If the answer is no – moving on, no worries, life is too short, and I think it is time I have the best year of my life – liberated and loved. Learned in 2015. Implemented just a few months later.*

Love all My Children

Little's love
Isn't small
It's larger
More forgiving
Overwhelming
Heart felting

Tiny fingers
All ten toes
Perfection
Just ask me
I'm mom

First
Smile
Hug
Step
Major accomplishment
Words become sentence
Even when the oldest's
Was: I said No.
As he backed up to the TV
knowing Mom
Had said no to playing
With the television
Creative Curious Carlin

Sleep deprived
Laughter not
Here comes number two
More joy
Christopher entered on a June evening
Three weeks early
Impatient ever since
In a hurry to be all
Grown up
Lover of animals
People and underdogs

Both brilliant
In their own ways
And those ways
Went down different
Paths
So very different
Little bodies
Minds
Emotions
Beliefs
Bones
They grew every night
Stretching out of
Clothes
Beds
Shoes
Rooms

Mother's patience
But never my love

Family expanded
Blending more
Into the mix
Heart grows
Protecting
Feeding
Explaining
Discovering
Home working
Loving
Traveling
Graduating
Graduating
Graduating
Graduating
Moving out

Alone
Quiet
No animated conversation
Over dinner
No debates
Loves shared
Snuggles and stories
Popcorn movie nights
Dominoes and cards

Performances
Sports
All missed
Grown
Up
And
Gone
Always loved
Every finger and toe
And I said: No

In the Darkness of Night

The neighbor's light
Burst on in the silent
darkness
Indented footprints revealed
In the snow
Seemingly emanating from no where
Leading to nothing
Yet here they are
In a Y pattern
Up since 4:00 wondering
Why myself
Built a fire
coffee dripping
Staring
Reading poems
Snippets of wisdom and nonsense
Do I have a fire for life
In my belly
Considering the whys
Of what I do
Think
Say
Make
Why feeding people
Is sharing Love
Has been since grandma

Made biscuits reaching from her wheelchair
Stirring
Flour dust in the air
Wheeling around her kitchen
Never complaining
To feed us her warm buttery
Love
Hers and Jesus' too
Equally loving yet
Independent of the chair
And religion
Grandma Mae grimaced
sipped her bourbon
Flicked her cigarette ashes
Teaching eleven year old
Me to can
Peaches
Pickles
Pears
You'll appreciate these
When winter comes.
She listened
Always she listened
And served up wisdom
In staccato sentences
You are good enough
Was a common theme
Here I sit thinking of the

Whys
Missing my grandma's and
Mom's laugh as we shared
A kitchen preparing our
Love
In the form of
Food to fill the belly
And the heart
Now food is so accessible
Microwave for six minutes
It's cold even when it's hot
Few understand it's
the love that's missing
The conversations
Sharing
Teachable moments
And I sit in the dark
Silent moments
Wondering why

Dreaming of Peace

I dream of a night when terror doesn't stalk our streets;
when fear doesn't pass through our consciousness
like a cold winter wind.

I dream of a time
When goodness overwhelms
Anger and joy defeats greed

In my prayer time
Closing my eyes while fully awake
I dream of families reunited through love
I dream of a day when there will be
No need of weapons to protect us from evil

I dream we lose the ravenous desire to watch killing
Both real and make believe
On electronic screens
Spending more time with our children
And our children's children creating memories
Of togetherness and hope

I dream a dream of peace and that it comes to us in our lifetime.

"Keep your heart open to dreams
For as long as there's a dream
There is hope, and as long as there is hope
There is joy in living." Anonymous

May all our dreams of joy and peace
For our families and the families
That we share this spinning planet with
Come true

Daughter Mother Sister Wife

Daughter mother sister wife
Puzzling pieces of my life
Seeking peace rather than strife
Debating the efficacy of an afterlife

Learning yearning burning with desire
A life lived upon a funeral pyre
In a world determined to be set afire
Tippy toeing on a high tight wire

Pleasing teasing smiles to bring
The tap dancing of a life in the ring
Dance like a butterfly upon the wing
Hopeful to recognize the real from bling

Reach teach preach the way
Make it through another day
Where is the power and who holds sway
Make everyone happy come what may

The joke yoke bespoke of a life delayed
While some might say a life well played
Life written upon a yellow pad laid
Amongst the many hours prayed

Who knew you amidst trees and blue skies
Would find love with your own brown eyes
Waking to seek my truth – rejecting lies
Morning poems written with deep sighs

The Circle of Grandmothers

The rattle of the needles
The clapping of the hands
The clucking of the tongues
The snapping of the bands
The circle of grandmothers
Pass me from lap to hand
Swirling in dance
Songs of life sung
Blessings well spoken
Pass it on make room for another
Daughter sister aunt or mother
Come join us in the light of the fire
Where hope is given
Wisdom shared
The warmth of femininity
The knowing of eternity
The matriarchs gathering
The circle of love unbroken

Mother's letter on my 16th Birthday.

Today you are sixteen. In the coming years you will be making choices and decisions. Some of those will not be easy…we tried to educate you in as many areas of life so that you can make a free choice as to which areas you want to pursue.

We taught you to question rather than accept…

You have always been encouraged to express your opinions. We didn't always agree but you in turn were willing to hear us out.

Don't ever become so grown up that you lose sight of simplicity. Don't take life or yourself so seriously that you forget to be happy, or silly or even childlike once in a while.

Accept people as individuals. This would be a very dull world if everyone were the same color, had the same dreams, the same ideas. We can all learn from each other.

Among other bits of wisdom she closed with have a joyous sixteenth year. Keep discovering, keep asking, keep caring.

With lots of love, Mother

The Family Dinner

I suppose most families are the same
You have the open-hearted ones
Greeting everyone at the door
Happy, glad to see one and all
There's always room for more
You also have cousin Jim or Dirk
who can't be bothered
To even look up from his perch

You can count on the care takers
Cuddling and diaper changing
Babies and great grandma
Smiling ones cooking and laughing
Trying to engage
The one wondering
Why all these people are bugging her
Eyebrows at alert
Daring anyone to speak to them
While they look down and away

The gushing aunts
Cheek pinching grandmas
Those who expect to be pinched
Running for cover
The grumpy that complain
Nonstop of the too cold or hot...

Someone get me a blanket
No turn on the air it's stuffy in here
The nonstop babbling of the one
Who just has so much to share
You're pretty sure they would talk
To the mirror if no one else is there

You have the one lifting everyone up with
A pat on the back or kind word
Smile waning as she sighs,
Sighting the one determined
To steal her joy
A shot of sarcasm or rolling eye
The bellicose uncle burping
Temporarily silencing
Those engaged in witty conversation
Sneered at from a distance
By the one who never lifted a finger
Or their voice to join in

Conversation continues into the night
With those cleaning up, those who are just pleased
To be together and the one who can't help
Because it would mess up their nails.
And at party's end
You have hugs and kisses by those that were truly present
Missing those who never arrived
Even though their chair was full
Sure their surly behavior was justified

By the inane babble of the ignorant family
They were forced into
By a nasty trick of fate

Some snuck out without a word
Not even a mumbled thanks
Others lingered on the porch not anxious to leave
A few huddled in the warmth of a family group hug
And as the hostess waves
Her last goodbye
She asks of no one in sight
What a great family dinner that was – right?
Turning to realize she's the only one
There as the house lights are turned out
Right?
She whispers into the silence of the night
Next time I'll fix salmon
They'll all love the salmon

Sammie

That moment
When you realize the most
Observant person in the house
Has four legs
She doesn't miss
A thing
She senses my moods
Oh, you don't feel well
Stay in bed
I won't leave your side
She lies by my side for hours
I feel her tender eyes upon me
Not even a whimper from her
Hubby has to pick her up to carry her away
Duty done
She's back – I am her person

She knows where everyone
Is at all times
Matt's coming home
She sounds the trumpet
Welcome home
Yaaaaaay
Aren't you excited
He's almost here

Can you see him yet
I know he's driving up the road

We don't have much of a schedule
But, Sammie has an internal one
Time for walk, cuddle, breakfast, outside
Relax, walk, dinner, outside, play time, relax
Come along – yeah you
Last time out
Now it's time for bed
She stands
At the stairs tail waggin
Wasn't this fun

What I still have — hope

I used to have
Father
Sister and Mother
Brother
In law
Dearest "punny" one
Artist sweetheart teacher
More than one loving preacher
Aunts and Uncles a plenty
Of the elders only two remain
I know my life will never be the same
Yet, friends and family gather round
Newness enters
Life goes on
Friendly faces
Now sit in their places
Love continues to flow
My heart stretches to grow
I realize all that seemed important
No longer holds the same sway
I no longer need to have it my way
Can't hold on fast
To anyone from the past
Life in these bodies does not last
The love though
Still

Rises with each morn
All those who passed my way
Rise up to greet every new day
Then fade back into my heart
As each morn is a new start
Swallowing tears
Of the memories of the years
Smiling at the wonder
Of a life anew
For me and for you
What adventures and joys
New territory did you discover
I think of the stories you'll tell
Father, Mother, Sister, Brother
When once we meet again
To greet the morning sunshine
Together

Love is an action Verb

Vowing
Promising
Mean nothing without the doing
Love is an action verb

Wishing
Wanting
Get little done without choosing
Love is an everyday choice

Prayers
Meditations
When filled with faith and hope
Love grows

Hugs
Kisses
Affection includes doing the dishes
Love lives by its own example

Truthful
Honest
Conversation that fills the heart
Love speaks words that heal

Laughter
Tears

Cherishing all that we are
Love laughs and cries – sometimes at the same time

Family
Memories
accepting and respecting who we are
Love expands to embrace them all

The Tug of Family

As I was searching for pictures for my sister's Memorial slide show, I found myself standing and staring at photographs displayed on my mother's wall of three generations that preceded my matriarchal grandmother. As I stood there I became transfixed, I recognized this family I never met. Time felt like it stood still and I pleaded for it to continue and I heard them say: There will be a day soon, soon enough when you will not have to ask...

The tug of family
Roots, memories
Running deep
Pulling me in
To memories
Not my own

Looking at the pictures
Of family long ago
I recognize something of myself in the gestures
The eyes and countenance
How I wish
That I knew them, yet
I sense their presence
The touch of a familial cord
Right now in this moment
Time does not exist

I want to hold on
To this precious moment
I call out
Stay with me
Just a while longer
But, no
Like a freight train
With car
After heavily laden car
Rumbling through my soul
They are gone
They were, after all
 just passing through

Like a whistle in the distance
Comes a still soft voice
There will be a day
Soon, soon enough
When you will not have to ask
And the cord will once again
Tug

Roots and memories
Running deep
With memories
Intertwined with your own

Grandmother's Wisdom

Reminiscing about my Grandma Mae as I sit in the early morning eating rye crisps, tuna, green olives and dill pickles. It was the rye crisp that got me thinking. Grandma was a non-conformist, great cook, whiskey drinking, Bay Area restaurant owner; a wise, outspoken feminist before there was such a thing. Grandpa was a wanderer, traveling the world looking for that next great thing, leaving his wife to single parent three children more often than not. In my adolescence Grandma lived at our house. She was my idol, confidant and friend. She was my defender and deflector when Dad was drunk and I was the object of his rage. She was my advisor in matters of the heart when Mom was working to support our family.

Coming home in my 8th grade year, feeling rejected, Grandma sat me by the fire and we had one of our talks – I told her of a boy I liked and I thought he was way too good for me. She looked at me with that knowing look, head tilted, cigarette about to spill its ashes, and said: "Oh honey, he goes to the bathroom just like everyone else. No one is ever too good for you!" Ashes flicked in the fire, hug given, I giggled, subject closed – but never forgotten. Whenever I have an issue, job or idea – or deal with a person that seems impossible, I remember Grandma Mae. I still hear her throaty laugh when I encounter a self-important person who thinks they are better than anyone else. Restroom is just down the hall. Thank you, Grandma.

We're keeping June

Crusty
Caring
Richard
Cousin by marriage
Who said to me
Nelson's gone but
We're keeping you
Forthright
Matter of fact
And now who's keeping Richard
Wife June says God is
Many hours
Laughing
Sharing wine
Meals
Music
Such fun and healing times
Two brothers and a cousin
All gone
Now it's three widows
Me, then Jan and now June
Of course we're keeping June

The Many Roles of the Other

Six years cancer. Love grew. Widowed.

Gate keeper
Caretaker
Nose wiper
Temperature monitor
Feeder
Lover
Reader
Responsibility responder
Silent Crier
It's not fair sobber
Compassion giver
Researcher
Phone caller
Special foods cooker
Protector
Refuse to be nagger
Pill cup filler
Insurance understander
Caterer
Listener
Comforter
Kindness sharer
Visitor Greeter
Cleaner

Pillow fluffer
Laundry doer
Smiler
Encourager
Reminder
Driver
Loader
Hugger
Holder
Partner
Buffer
Explainer
Massager
Hand squeezer
Pray-Er
Bill payer
Shopper
Kindness thanker
Hair comber
Bandage and creams applier
Foot rubber
Dumb joke teller
Laugher
Cleaner
Observer
Sigher
Memory storer
Well wisher replier

Trash emptier
Exhausted sleeper
Night time watcher
Wouldn't have it any other way-er
Compelled by love, giver and receiver

Meeting or Homecoming

Wondering
Wandering
Window shopping
Stopping to gaze
Into each other's
Face
    Do I know you
Eyes
    Yes I do
Mirroring
Capturing reflections
Sharing
    Beauty in the boats upon water
    Composition and colors
    Nature
    Sea
    Rocks
    Ideas and thoughts
No need to impress
Be impressed
No awkward moments
Instead

Taking hands
Touching hearts
Lips

Minds
Eyes gazing
To the sea
Into the soul
Met
Found
Are you going so soon
You just got here

They say it takes a
Lifetime
And perhaps it did
bringing us to this place
To discover the yearning experienced
The desire growing
To yet be fulfilled
In the homecoming of our hearts
In just a few hours

Circle of Friends

In my circle of friends, we often talk about living out our purpose in life. I am wondering if we may spend too much time worrying if we have "done" our one big purpose, losing sight of all the important things that we have been doing along the way.

While I actually know what my purpose is, I don't always know how to accomplish every detail. I continue to plug away, and along the way I do other things — some important to only me, or a few others, some important to others and not in any large way a part of what I see as my purpose, and some things just must be done as a necessity of living. On further reflection, maybe I am blinded to the fact that my life is my purpose and whatever I am learning, loving and doing may just be what, and who I am supposed to be. Perhaps, "it" is all about how we act and the attitude we hold no matter what we are doing. Love

Poetry and Photography with Friends

These next two poems are compilations of my words with friends on Facebook who responded to my poetry prompts. And my friend Deb Bradford, who posts a daily photograph of such immense beauty, graciously allowed me to share some here.

Diving into the depths of love

Sandy memories running through my fingers
Abrading my heart as it polishes my soul
Salt tears on my cheek, transform into a grateful smile
Each grain, a smile, a tear, a gentle touch all fleeting Inspiration
but not the less an imprint on my heart
Comes the dawn.
Low lying fog
Water that cozies up to the shore and then recedes.
Everything outside this window is my schoolbook
reminding me, comforting me, instructing me
These are the ways of the earth
Follow and you will be at ease.
Comes the early morning hours, the clarion call of work and play.
If you are one of the wise and fortunate ones, they are the same thing.
Look to the day's path, take your first step with eager joy.
Like the hours we've run and slept through,

The meals shared secrets held
And as the tides,
like the moon,
wax and wane,
so, too, may the good memories flow and the rest ebb away...
My thoughts linger to the sound of waves on the sand,
Peacefully knowing our kindred spirits listen
The sandy grains of memory will linger, returning to illuminate
my dreams.

Robbed of Hugs

*During Covid 19, Shelter in Place, I asked my friends what they
missed the most.*

Missing most
The touching
Feel and exuberance
Of the common hug
The embrace that says hello
All is well
Goodbye I'll miss you
The gentle hug
Hearty bear hug
The child's sweet snuggle
The warmth and joy of loving family
Playing games
Sharing cinnamon toast
Tater tots
Simple pleasures
Touch
Community
Now keeping distances
Friends pass as strangers
Nothing but a nod
No friend's hand to help
Heal the heartaches
From the loss of our loved ones

Gone too soon
It's always too soon
Moms
Dads
Dearly beloveds
The emptiness of
The other side of the bed
The door locked
To our grown up
Babies they'll
Always be our babies
Kisses now blown through
Cold glass
Moss and trees
Bird song
Our freedom to roam
Now limited to home
Yearning to hold
What we can only imagine
Travel banned
No hearing of
The sound of Coquis
Singing songs
Keeping rhythm
with the tin roof percussion
Of falling rain in Puerto Rico

If You Know Me

If you know me
You know people
Always come before
Ideologies
Politics
Religions
I appreciate all
The gorgeous shades
Skin
Hair
Eyes
I don't care
Where you were born
Or where you're going
I want to know you
That beautiful human
That you are
The person inside
That lights you up
The other definitions
Labels
Names
Affiliations
Matter little at all.
Your story does matter
What makes you

Laugh
Cry
Sing
Dance
Create
What do you love
Deeper than the ocean
What inspires you
To fly beyond any confines
Of titles or monies
Who are you
What brings you joy?

We Have a Lilac Festival

Even when no lilacs bloom
The festival of lilacs
Is in the village
Friend Judith, rallies
All our spirits
With her infectious optimism
Yes, it's raining but never
On her parade
and we march
Happily alongside her
Thankful, for her sunny attitude
To warm our hearts

Some friendships are bolstered
By the internal joy
Shared from the heart
of a remarkable friend
The one who doesn't give up
She conjures up a smile
Even when she's exhausted
Encouraging the discouraged
Humbly never telling us what to do

While she quietly is
Lightening
Our load

Not allowing us to implode
And with complete trust
we'll follow Judith's
Lead
Because
She loves us

So off we go
Grumbling
Mumbling
Stumbling
Laughing and sharing
Stretching ourselves
To match the potential
and beauty she sees in us
As we go
Back to the lilac festival
Just to bask in her light
Again.
Is that snow?

Today

Today I feel the pull to
Gentleness
Silence
Kindness
Today
I will be exceedingly
Quiet
Listening
Hearing the sighs
In the trees
The song of the birds
The joy of my heart
Before there is no more
Today I will be with
Those with losses
Of loved ones
Of hope
Of desire
Of wellness
Who cry in the night
I'm sensing
Some of you are
With me in this need
To be gentle and not
Allow another's
Anger

Rage
Threats
From yesteryear
Or today
To enter our heart and mind
Today I will be kind
I will remember who
I am
Why I'm here

The Gardener and the Garden

You are
The gardener
And the garden
Dear friend
Sprouting
Growing
Wild
Spirit of a thousand
Breezes
Dandelion fluff
Blowing
Into fertile soil
Escaping upon the wind
Rejoined with source
To take root
Another day

My Love for LIAV Camp

Thank You, Patti Digh and Mary Anne Em Radmacher
And all the tribe of Creatives

My eyes burn brightly
My mind is awash with joy
I'm still on camp time

Orange red golden
Poems fall fallen falling
Fresh memories float

Upon the water
Reflections mirror my thoughts
Recreating tribe time

Seeing faces smile
Hugs felt tears shed open arms
Capturing moments

Girlfriends are the best

How many girlfriend
Times are too
Often
Too long
Not long enough
You know you'll
Come away
Happier for the day
Refreshed
Reminded
Reassured
You are appreciated
They are loved
You've shared your story
Listened to theirs
No judgments made
No beds either
You can have coffee
In jammies
Or dress up for
A girls night out
We love our others
The spouses, kids
Parents too
But girl friends;
Are the best

How can you have only one
Best friend
When each friend
Is unique
You relate on different issues
You grow in separate ways
Cycling back together
As if never apart
Facebook
FaceTime
What's app
Were all made for
Girlfriends

In These Days

In these days
Exercising my restraint
Muscles strengthening
To not become
The worst of me
Practicing kindness
Stretching my silences
Yet, I have that shadow
That wants to convince
Everyone of my truth
Even if that means
Wielding heavy doses of guilt
Shaking my finger
Proving wrong
Those who think differently
Than me
How can you be so blind…
Oh no – there I go
Stop
Pause
Breathe
This road is a dead end
No life to be found here
Turn around
And find the better side of me
To be Kind
Considerate
Humbled

The colors of love

The colors of love
Light up
Our lives

Boundless love
Crosses rivers
Crests mountains

To shine on us all
Expanding our human heart
To include

All the colors of the rainbow

Hopeful

Lists are made
Carefully thought about
What are the traits
Talents, characteristics
Of the person the universe
Has picked out
Not just will he please me
But will I please him
Is it possible
There could be one
Breathing the thought of him
In hopeful anticipation
All things considered
No settling for less

Nice people met
Yet...
No one right
And...
No one really wrong
Intuition speaks out
You know the answer
Keep believing for
One
Who softly
Enters

Quietly smiling
Knowingly
He floats into view
With his eyes he says
Were you waiting for me?
...I've been hoping for you

So Now They've Proven

What we knew all along
The heart speaks
The cells talk to the brain
What the heart desires
The mouth speaks
Greatest commandment
Love the Lord
Your God
With all your heart
Soul
Mind
And your neighbor
As yourself
Let the heart speak
Love
Gratefully to our source
Thankfully for our neighbors
With appreciation for who we are
Let our heart swell
With joy filled
Wonder for all we have
 and are being
Scientifically proven
What we already knew
The heart communicates
And it's up to us what it says.

True Love

True love…
Rare
Precious
Not to be wasted
Some would say
Yet…
When it is shared
Like the loaves and fishes
Given freely
Love expands
Growing and multiplying
Coming full circle
To the heart
Of the giver
Nourished by love's
Life giving force

Unconditional love…
The joy of which
Can't help but spill over
A fountain of life
Colors flowing
Expanding outward
Rushing inward
Felt in the deepest regions
Heart, mind and body

Recognized
Visible
Palpable
Breathing life
Affirming joy
Into the soul

A poem of paradoxical proportions

Loving others is not free
It comes with a price
Everything you have, are, or will ever be
For true love is only found when you relinquish the right to be right
With its companions; condemnation and what about me-me-me
Paradoxically though, love must start in the heart of the me
For only when we have expelled our inner critic, pointing to all
our faults
Learned to accept self and love who we are; just as we are
Can we truly be free to let go of criticizing the other
Only then can the light expand, embrace, and grow into we
Unstoppable waves of loving kindness, acceptance, joy, and
grace turned out to be
Worth the price for love between you and me

Sickness a weakness

A cold and asthma has kicked in
I hate to admit
I consider sickness, a weakness
In my self – I do not permit

It gets in the way
Of plans for the day
Inconvenient and stressing
It robs of the blessing

For this, I have no time
I'm in bed making really poor rhyme
I ask, when there is so much to do
How could you let this happen to you?

Judging myself an inferior creature
I thought you were a positivity teacher
Meditate and pray it away
Listen here body – to what I say

Be well, live in the light
Stop coughing in the middle of the night.
Sleeplessness, frustration only makes it worse
I hate being ill – it is a curse

Feeling guilty, not to do my part
On projects that only got a start
I love you no matter what you do
My sweet man says – Let me take care of you

Unaccustomed to being the cared for
Pride and hair mussed, throat sore
Revealing exhaustion on my face
I wrap up in the comforter and accept love's embrace

I hear him whisper, be well
A God shiver, makes my heart swell
I am well, and soon my body will agree
Blessed, not cursed by the one who loves me.

In gratefulness for the kindness of dear ones

Gratitude for Kindness

Grateful for every kind act
Every whisper of soothing word
Unexpected gesture
Gift of time
Sweetness in sorrow
Loving acceptance
Shared breath of silence
Thankful for the hearty

Laugh in the face of defeat
Astringent upon the sting of failure
Acknowledgement of triumphs
Of any size, sort, attempt to soar
It is the feel of kindnesses
Both given and received
that I remember most

How Often Do We Settle

How often do we settle
Or accept something less
Than perfect
Because it's here
Available
Easy
How often do we think
We settled yet it was choice
After all
How often do we see
Answers to questions
Not yet asked
Do we question our
Decisions berating ourselves
For each choice if it doesn't
Seem to work out
I read my journal written in NY
I was 25
Angry
Hungry for answers
Not willing to be patient
Now damn it I want answers
Now
So I settled I decided
There were no positive
Answers therefore

Take what's here
There's nothing better
I refused to wait
If I wait I might miss out
Later when regret
Flooded in
I did it again

Does One Person Make a Difference

Does one person make a difference
One Lover
Friend
Child
Mother

A single person can touch my life
Reach in and calm the strife
Sisters of the heart
Distance and time can't tear us apart
Brothers of the soul
Make me smile... add to the whole

Life isn't meant to be performed solo
One note upon another
Joining together in a crescendo
Playing in harmony
Highs and lows
Creating a lyrical life symphony

Caught Myself Judging Another

Judging another's behavior
Sadness crept over me
Humbled as I considered
I ever thought I knew the answers
Presumed to understand the will
Or won't of Heaven

If I've ever boxed you up
Called you a nasty name
Said you were evil
Questioned if you prayed
Attempted to take your freedom
To be who you are
Please...forgive me

If you've ever felt
I judged you
Unworthy
Unlovable
Unforgivable
Unsuitable
Please...know I am sorry

If it helps
Whatever injustice I afflicted
You with — I inflicted
On me too

May you know

It's a tense and shaky time and it's also our one precious life.

May you know
That you've been
Seen
Heard
Valued
May you know
That you've been
Loved
Cherished
Respected
May you know
That you've made a
Difference
Impact
Change
for good
May you know
You will never be forgotten

No word for love...

There is no word for
The depth
Density
Luminosity
Of love
Intimacy that flows in secret places
Love like desire
What shallow intractable words
Volumes of poems written
Do no justice
They skim along the surface
Barely causing a flutter
Go deep
Deeper still
Than the words
Could it be that no
Words
Compare
Explain
Lay bare
The truth of love
Soul mate
Love of my life
Twin flame
Lack the luster
Shine

The pop and sizzle
Come lie with me
Let our hearts beat as one
And we'll explore
What there is no word for

Kindness

Let kindness
Lead
As your words
Start to flow
Ask them
What is your motivation?
To prove you're right?
To cut and wound those you think are wrong?
To tear down another,
To make you feel better than?
Is your motive to bring peace?
To light another's way?
To bring a smile instead of frown?
To ease fear or increase its power?
Why speak at all?
This morning my jaw
Clenched
My heart ached
I wanted vindication
I asked my motivation
It was not kindness
I remained silent
Silence is not agreement
Nor is it argument
Trust that until
I know my motivation

It is better not to speak.
Do all things with love.
This is kindness to
My heart

Different Kinds of Happy

All kinds of lives
And times in lives
Provide opportunities
For different kinds of happy
There's the happy of skipping
Down the lane
With little hands held
The book read at night
To curious minds
Once upon a time...
The kiss of love
The hug of family
The creation of art
The words penned
Dishes done together
Song sung
Danced to the beat
Bubbles in the air
And bath
Rubber ducky
Friends gathered
Doggie's sweet gaze
Dinner time
Smell of trees
Fall leaves
Salty breeze

Camp fire
Popcorn
New car
Babies' breath
Baking bread
Cinnamon
Lemon grass
Fresh ground coffee
Before it's brewed
Starlight sunlight moonlight too
Walks
Talks
Memories spoken
Snuggles
Clean sheets
Smiles laughter giggles
I'm sure you could add a few
Of the many ways
To be glad
Grateful
Happy

Seeing Beyond
the Finite:
My Love Affair
With
Image

Please accept that this is my love story, you have your own.

Years ago, the subject of being a believer came up. Are you a Christian or just spiritual? I was asked. Not feeling judged, or criticized, the question prompted me to respond that I don't have all the answers but, that I personally know God, it's a relationship. I don't see God as a patriarchal father figure for me God is the Spirit, Truth, Love and Energy that speaks to our hearts. Thank goodness, it's personal, alive now. I don't have to be reliant upon a belief system or someone else's words or experiences. I feel no compunction to defend what I know. I have been touched by love. I experience and see God's love. I was not satisfied to have a long-distance relationship – it was to be up close and personal, or not at all. As a young skeptic, I resonated with "Come reason with me" and I did and do. Hours, weeks, months, years, of pouring through Greek and Hebrew and multiple all-nighters to discover the definition of God is much deeper, different, bigger, better, universal, than what I ever thought of in my finite mind. The Creative Expanding Spirit isn't limited by our thoughts or beliefs. I know, God's Love did not quit being present to us because some men compiled some letters and documents into a book and proclaimed it done. Please accept that this is my love story, you have your own. Everyday love is born in my heart, every day is Christmas to me.

I Am Light

In my prayers and meditations, I sometimes experience visions and dreams. In this one some years ago — I saw all forms of religious sects, denominations, dogmas, and ideas dumped into a shoebox, as the last one went into the box they all swirled together turning into thick gray cement. Under the immense weight of it all, I saw the box sink further and further down into a large, deep, rapidly flowing river, going straight down to the bottom and the voice in my heart spoke:

I Am Light.
I am not all these laws and fears.
I Am Light.
I Am everything, and weigh nothing.
I Am Light.

Wind. Love. God.

We know the wind by the trees
sighing the dust blowing
waves crashing,
kites flying,
hats and rooftops being whisked
away by the invisible.

In the stillness when it's gone.

We know love through acts of
kindness, generosity, passion,
empathy and compassion,
feelings of joy,
desire to protect and serve.

In the emptiness when it's missing.

We know God, in a thankful,
overflowing heart,
in the unconditional love we experience,
in acts of creativity,
in the peace that calms the storm.

In the void when it seems there are no answers for the pain in life.

These three are not visible,
or tangible except by the reaction

to their presence.
When the wind is still,
the focus of our love is not present,
or we do not hear God speak,

Is that enough to prove they do not exist?

Or could it be the evidence,
the reason we question their veracity
because, at some point we have
knowledge or experience of the wind,
love and God?
How else would we know
when their presence is not being felt.

In My Knower

In my knower, the place that resides in the depths of my soul, I understand things so profound that my brain shakes my head in wonder of it all.

No need to defend what I know I stand silent in the presence of the powerful, beyond comprehensible, knowing.

Picking up the transmissions of angelic messages whispered into the hearts of humankind – You are loved. You are loved. You are loved. Yes, even you, with all your flaws, and unbelief, you are loved. This I know, in my knower and it cannot be disproved, because it is not a theory or belief system it is my experience, it is known to me personally.

I am loved
I am loved
I am loved unconditionally
with all my imperfections
and unbelief.
This I know.
Not because any book told me so…

Overcoming Darkness

Darkness like a dense
Swirling fog
Seeks to dim
The light

The fog of
Fear
Jealousy
Distrust
Sweeps in to snuff
Out the light
The light fears not
Light is
Always was
Never ends

Where the light is
No darkness
Can prevail
Says the Word
Listen
See the truth
Let the light of love flow
Dissipating all else

If you look with the eyes
That do not see
But know
The eyes that see beyond
The physical realm
To that place of heart
The light shines
Brightly
It never quits
Only our perceptions
Where darkened
Thoughts veiled the beauty
Revealed the temerity
The momentary lapse
Of truth
The singular second of
Breath held
Before the light
Floods back in
With the inhale
All else flees in
The exhale
The light that never left
Shines
Once again and forever
Vowing
To always love
See the light

In the darkness
Breathe through
The fear
Name it
See it
Letting it go
With a thankful sigh
Of farewell
Acknowledging any wisdom
Releasing any emotion
Accepting the light of love
That floods into the void created
When darkness is overcome

Life is a Prayer

My life is a prayer
Praying unceasingly
Speaking out loud
Is being the living prayer
Compassion
Love
Peace & Mercy
Creativity's joy
I choose my prayer
Daily with gratitude
I am not what happens
I am not a victim
I am a prayer
Whatever we ask for we receive
What we give our attention
Is our prayer
Fear or love
Unwittingly or not
I am the prayer
The living prayer

God Experiences

My life is full
of God experiences.
My collected memories
Happenings
Actualities
Arising from
Listening
Observing
Learning

Wisdom from the experiencing
Hand in fire,
I learned fire is hot.
Hand in God's hands
I learned trust
In life's
  Pain
    Loss
      Fear
        Death
          Sorrows

Learning how
I live and love matters
In a picture I cannot fully frame
Not everything known to mankind

Is all there is.
Accepting that not all things
Can or need be
Explained
Understood
Defended
By the finite human mind
I can never say I know
the mind of God
Yahweh
Breath of Life
Spirit
Truth
I can only share my experience
That for me God is
All encompassing love
    universal
      multi-versal
      and more
My sense is that we
We're given the example
Loving
Trusting
Giving
Up our "right to be right"
Making room for differences
To love our planet and all humanity

In the silence of the soul

In Silence
Seeking
Sighing
Sitting

In Silence
Shining
Seeing
Soaring

In Silence
Sipping
Sensing
Savoring

In Silence
Serving
Supporting
Sanctifying

In Silence
Surrendering
Simplifying
Signing

In Silence
Awaken my soul

Let me see
What is yet to be
Silently revealed

The Miraculous

I asked
For the Miraculous
For truly only
That would do
The miraculous is always
Something beyond what you
Can see a way to do
Blind
I'd run out of tricks
My hat was empty
I asserted, reworked, finessed
Finally took my hands
Off
Let go
OK I'm willing to give up
I'm willing
To give
To give
It up
It up
It up
Perhaps I'm asking
For things not
Meant to be
Not in the cards for me
But oh how I wish

It was
It was
It was
Three requests
You see
None of them possible
Not possible for me
To accomplish
Work out
Make happen
Silently
No drums beating
Not even appearing
Magically miraculous
Eyes fill with tears
I'm here
Answer to one
Arrives from a friend
Number two from words shared
Slowly opportunities appear
And three in a phone call
All answered
Like the salesman on TV
But, wait there's more
Now here's the difference
From what we ask and what
We receive
Answers to questions

Not fully thought out
I wake up to see
Miracle four and five
From unusual sources
Make themselves known
The miraculous isn't done
Answers are often not
What I would have thought
The parting of the sea
As the Egyptians close in
A Rumi poem
When my heart
Is seeking solace
I had only to listen
To open my eyes
To receive

Realization Floats

The realization floats upon the water
Splashing accidental pigment
Later to become a part of the whole
I hear words...the music is in the heart
The song in the soul
We don't always know from where it came
Not everything seen or known to mankind
Is all there is.
Mysteries even Einstein couldn't solve
Why photons are particle and waves
How observing anything changes its
Trajectory in life
Accepting that not all
Can or need be
Explained
Understood
Defended
By the finite human mind
In the living is the inevitable dying
In order to be rebirthed
In the song is the final chorus
The last stroke on guitar
The paint dries
Creation. Life. Death. Love.
Beautiful planet
Perhaps never to be fully framed

We are a work in layers
Always in progress
Sometimes set aside
Stopped
But, do we ever know when it's finished
The Creative works on
eyes open eyes closed
The music never stops
Continues expanding
and it's OK
That I do not know how or where
But I know in my heart song that it does

Life Lessons

Learning lessons
Running scales
Ruminating
It takes repetition
To build a psychic memory
Muscles to remember
Find our way home
Practice makes...
Well, not perfection
I suppose it's more about what we
Practice

    Kindness
    Goodness
    Compassion
    Helpfulness

    Bullying
    Shaming
    Rudeness
    Selfishness

We are what we do the most
We are the actions we take
We are the words we speak

Who's God's Mommy

Why do I exist
Who am I
To speak words
To be heard
Seeking answers
Gazing into the night sky
What is the purpose
Of Mother Earth
Father Sun
Brother Wind
Sister Moon
Who is the voice speaking to my heart

Listen
Be still and breathe in life
Pay attention to the details
The beauty in the blossom, leaf, bird, brush stroke,
smoothness of warm woods, light upon the water
Seek the beauty of truth
Create the kindness you receive
Be your authentic, unique self
Love everything that makes you…you
Even what you don't understand
Forgive yourself any shortcomings you perceive
Forgive others too
Let go of pain

See it drip from your fingers
Speak words of affirmation

Reach to the stars
Know that you are loved
Hear the eagle cry
Water flow
Wind blow
Feel the wave of inspiration
Dance upon the waters
Celebrate this moment in life
And the next and the next

Who are you I cry
Must I know the
Who and why
Before I live or die
Does it matter
If it's just so
If I knew.
What could I do
Would I
Should I
Change
Earth sun wind and moon
The answer's no.
Yet I seek the creator's
Meaningful purpose
To give my life a reason

To be me
Amongst the many yous
So many whys
swallowing up
My life in the asking
 Is it me
Wanting to take control
Looking into space
To find my own face
Is it God I want to replace
I've not the slightest notion
How to run an ocean
Not the vaguest plan
For what to do with the land
Then why the whys
Of who's God's mommy
Is it all just curiosity
Why do I have this desire
To know who
Created the heart that beats
The air I breathe
The love
The hurt and ire
The frozen tundra
The warmth of fire
If I'm to love you
Who are you

Is this a blind date

I've Been to the Center of the Sun

I've been to the center of the sun
As I entered anger burned away
Then went self righteousness
I'm right and you're wrong flamed
Out of sight
All physical ownership disappeared
Everything that made me think
There is value here
Everything that is but, the real me
The me at my core
Met the sun at her center
With all else burned away
We laughed and danced audaciously
To the loving song of forever

The Lost Word

*Is there any surprise that I woke at 2:20 this morning dreaming
that I had lost the word to end my poem? The word was in a white
square, the whole poem was snow white. The word was missing and
I hunted everywhere. I woke and I'd found my word, it was bough.
Now I have no idea what the rest of the poem was. Sleepless snowy
nights, all covered in white.*

The importance of a word
Strung together
A thought
Plan
Vows
Speech
Manifesto
Address
Mystery novel
Biography
Memoir
Einstein's quotes
theatrical TV movie script
Sentences that change your life
    Sorry, you have lymphoma
    Will you marry me
    You got the job
    We are making cuts
    Mom, I joined the army

Dad, I quit school
Sit down honey...
In the beginning was the word
All things came into being
By the power of the
Word

I Do not Pretend to Understand

In my quest for peace, I don't deny the importance of passion, tears, or anger at injustice.

I'm learning to be grateful for all human experiences, not just the miracles or happy times. But, also those that are difficult.

It is in pain that compassion and love can grow with a deeper desire to eradicate the cause of the distress.

The agony of injustice against people in the colonies gave rise to a new free country, later recognizing injustice still existed brought laws to insure freedom for all peoples – even we women finally got the right to vote. But, it didn't come easily, there was pain along the way – still is.

Cancer stealing lives, brings research for healing (not just more drugs) and hope for a healthy life.

Violence, on our streets, brings people together to find answers to the deepest needs (not just more jails).

I do not pretend to understand why we need these painful lessons in the first place. I am beginning to understand that when suffering comes —look for what good may ensue, what answers there could be for today and tomorrow that hopefully will make life better for those that follow.

Chameleon

I woke from a dream where I was trying to make everyone happy by becoming whatever they needed.

The chameleon
Changes color shape texture
To fit into an environment
Shape shifter
Disappearing into the background
Don't look at me
If you can't see me I'm safe
Said every
Abused person
Everywhere

Life Lived on Social Media

My advice: don't try to sleep after reading posts and comments on posts that display a lack of human-kindness. I wrote this and then had to meditate and pray to bring my heart beat to normal.

When your heart is sad
And you feel you cannot speak
Blame bounces on the tongue
But you know you will
Swallow the bitterness

Words spoken in haste
Can create regret
lived out in social media
With truth dangling nearby
Cut off in the edited version

Rumors and rumors of rumors
Running amok
You know "those" people
The they of they and them
Said so – it must be true

Bar talk spoken in inebriation
Gossip masquerading as requests
In prayer groups and bible studies
Words used in judgment
Each sentence a jab to the heart

Opposing opinions shared
Hate
Threats
Disappointment on all sides
Spilled out on Facebook
instantly grammed

Prayers against someone
Prayers to protect another
Me, I'll pray for truth.
Truth to be spoken, truth
Where is the truth to be written

Don't just pray or offer good thoughts
Send help, donations to the wounded
Feed the poor, broken or victims
Of man or nature created violence
And of course still voice your prayers to heal

I cannot pray to protect lying
I cannot defend those who bully
I also cannot make right those
Who hate the haters
They've now become

Can you imagine a world without hate?
I pray for it daily.
I speak of it often
And I know someone will even take offense at that.

Yes, my heart is sad
Please, when tempted to rally
Against another, any other
Blaming their beliefs or political party realize
That you dehumanize us all

If you hate Christians
Or non believers
Liberals or republicans
You group individuals into just
Two categories and divide us in half

To me hate is hate
I cannot condone hate.
Right left red blue
If it's hate you speak
You all sound the same to me

I can and do disagree
I defend your right to disagree
I know you feel justified
To feel that the bad of the other far outweighs yours

But hate foments more hate
Digging in to defend how
Right you are and the other guilty
Don't you realize bad people exist
They don't have a religion or party

Even they have a role to play
Drawing contrast to healing
Hating them will not change
Their minds it will only create
More walls of defense.

I don't mean we should accept
Harm to another
Those who would separate us
Seek to harm us all
There is bad I'm not Pollyanna
Use your energy to heal and create

Can you imagine a world without hate?
I pray for it daily.
I speak of it often
And I know someone will even take offense at that.

Up Praying for Truth

Up praying
For truth
Who has it
Who stole it
When did hyperbole become it
If I repeat lies
Do they magically become truths
Is a fact truth
Are there alternative facts
Three eye witnesses speak
What is true for them
Each believes they have it
If I believe it is it true
Is veracity spoken with alacrity
Angry words shoved in my face
Truth
I'm up praying for truth
Like a wave to flow
Over our country
Face it
Speak it
Lies make our face turn purple
Noses grow
Do we know
What is truth
I beseech it

I request it
I need it
To know what is true
Is it what we want
Or do we just want
To keep our jobs
Our friends
Our comfort
Our old standards
We swallow whole the lies
Because if we aren't who
We thought we were
Who are we
Can we even ferret out
The truth from amongst
All the partial truths
Half truths
Wish they were truths
If only it was easy to know what is true
If I wish long enough
Will water become wine
Lead turn into gold
How do you know
What truth feels like
Hubby wakes up
Is this a Katie Byron thing
He asks
He says this sounds a bit political

I respond
It depends on which side you're on
Me,
All I want is truth
Or do I
Is this a few good men
You can't handle the truth
Moment
I'm up praying for truth
And the ability to
Recognize it
Synthesize it
Memorize it
So I don't waiver
Or repeat a lie
My prayer
Come truth come
Holy Spirit hover over the chaos
Bring peace
Let truth rise

What cost kindness spoken

What cost
Kindness
Compassion
Truly seeing another
Before speaking

In just the moment it
Takes to slowly inhale
Weigh the cost
The words in your head
Don't always require an exit

If words written or spoken
Are to get even
Defend bad behavior
Accuse or judge
Better to leave them silent

If words wash wounds
Bring hope
Heal brokenness
Lift a spirit
Go ahead
Speak
    Expound
        Enlighten
In celebration of life

Moving forward from here

Stepping into the day
Not looking back
Moving forward from here
Here and this here
The now of where I am
Cannot be altered by
Retreating to former times
This is the me of this moment
And the next
I cannot return to wishing
I had taken better care
Body
Finances
Heart
This is who I am now
I can choose to like
Even love who I am
Or I can live in a past
That doesn't exist.
Me
I think I'll move forward
Not backward
From right here

Soap in the Mouth

I have a visceral
Response to cruelty
To name calling
Bullying
Slamming or shaming another
In defense of self to
Destroy
Defame
Demean with
Sarcasm meant to rip
Just to gain
Some sense of justification
Casually without remorse
Fanning flames of hate
And injustice
Building oneself up
By tearing others down
Not once sorry for the pain
The lies or acts
That as a child
And later parent
Still are not acceptable
Some of us would have been
Grabbed by the ear with
Soap stuck in our mouth
For speaking as some do

Now from podiums of power
Civility matters
Debate
All deserve respect and voice
We can agree to disagree
Without being met with rancor
Requiring apologies and forgiveness
Be kind
Act with compassion
Accept responsibility
Speak truth
My friends and family
My love for you crosses
Party lines
I know you all
Have hearts of love
When it comes to family
And the importance of friendship
This is not who we are
Especially as we celebrate
The Prince of Peace
And Festival of Lights

Watching the memorial for President Bush I was struck by the importance of the soldiers bearing the hefty weight of the casket.

Daddy, what did you do today?

Today, I carried the President
Today, I bore the weight
Of the man who bore
The weight of us all
I felt the responsibility
To do my best
Step carefully
Silently honor
Lift him up
As he lifted our country
Honored to be one of eight
Who carried the President
Humbled I'll continue to carry
The sense of love and service
I felt when
I carried the President today.

I've family members who died because of war.

Memorial Day

I yearn for the day
When we won't
Need to remember
To thank those
Who sacrificed their lives
To protect us from ourselves
For no sacrifice will
Be required
As the earth
Finds peace
Humanity
Finally becomes humane
Love prevails
People cease invading
Other's lands, minds, and faiths
We cease stealing other's
Resources, lives, children and hope
We learn the lesson of respect
Sharing love and kindness
Not just for those who look
Think or act
As we do
But for all
And wars will be no more

We can have a weekend to remember Goodness
To celebrate peace
Grateful we finally awoke
To realize a peaceful world
Where mankind is finally kind
The Universe, Angels and God
Will celebrate with us
That we finally
as a people
Grew up
And Gave up
Our selfish ways
For if we do
The greatest commandment
To love,
Respecting, and honoring others as we do ourselves
All the other rules and laws are fulfilled
But
Until that day
Thank you, to all those who loved Enough
To sacrifice their lives
For us to have the freedom
To pursue happiness
Follow any or no religion
Speak our minds without persecution
Be able to have hope in humanity
Govern ourselves peaceably
Learn to respect all of our citizens equally

Perhaps
It will yet come to pass
That with this freedom
The world and all
Its people
Will live out the greatest lesson
To love one another
Enough
To leave the stories of wars
In the history books

The Light Leaking

There have been days
when I haven't released much light
days regretfully I held it in tight
The light finds ways to leak
Cracks where it seeps
As revelation I seek
to reveal where darkness held
Me in pain and distress
Jesus said: ...my burden is light
he didn't mean as oft said
it wasn't too heavy a load
he meant it was the light of Love
That shines on and in all creation
We all need to be a bit more leaky
Let our love shine through
The places not so hardened
By hyperbole, judgment, anger
Resentments
Let love shine from the core

Is This Love

My one magnificent life
Is not determined
By Politics
Lies
Disagreement
Disappointment
I believe in love
Martin Luther King
The value of all humans
The gift of life on this planet
Not hate to change
Politics
Disagreement
Disappointment
Into Truth
Truth
We all have only one unique life
Ask yourself
Is this love
Did I say this with love
Did I listen with love
Did I act with love
If we ALL act with
LOVE
hate will dissipate
If you hear hate

Read hate
Write hateful disparaging words or
Think anyone isn't worthy of love
Kindness
Re check yourself
As you start to write
Ask yourself if your words will
Harm hurt hate
Or bring light to a life

Sometimes

Some days, sometimes and some things are floating in my mind.
Some days you wake to find your life and much of what you thought
you knew, are now,
not your reality. What you hoped for is long distant because in an instant
your hopes and dreams have taken on a new focus.
Hope not gone; just changed form.
Sometimes, my heart is bursting with love, faith and compassion
and still I cry.
Some things, can bring life's greatest joys; while others can rob the
life from you.
I have learned to seldom live in an always, never and ever state of
mind; because of some days, sometimes and some things that can
change your life at any time.
Staying open to the changes and looking for what good may come is
my way of keeping my sanity – sometimes.

Vision or Dream?

Five years ago, I had a powerful vision while not quite asleep and not really awake – I dreamt of walking towards an iridescent, shimmering ball of light; swirling and expanding. I calmly walked into the ball. Coming joyfully towards me were loved ones no longer here. My sister led the way, laughing, full of health, vibrant – gone five weeks ago, my husband Nelson, ten years ago today, just behind him, my Dad, eighteen years ago today, and my Grandmother, further back, over thirty years ago. I knew there were more, but these were the ones most clearly visible; all so very happy. Joy surrounded them, light infused them, they sparkled and then my sister spoke. "It was a role. I played my role and when it was done, I exited. Your role is not over, back to the stage with you."

Just a dream? I wonder…

The words spoken resonated with me. I always believed we each had a purpose, each playing a different role on this stage of life; heroine, villain, love interest, second banana, or in the chorus, all equally important to the story. Today's lesson for me: I'm to play my part well, enjoy the production, take direction, but not mindlessly. Think creatively about different ways of playing the role, in discussions with the director and other cast members. Learn my cues, spots and lines, even improvise. The story of life, is after all not all drama and tragedy but, also a romantic comedy! Wow, sigh, don't take myself so seriously. Yet, it is important to "show up" and not let the rest of the cast down. This role is not who I really am… soon it will be over. When I step off stage it will be into the loving arms of those who are living the real life in the lights!

Freedom in Letting Go...

There is a freedom
in letting go
that is totally different
than giving up.
Surrender isn't always
defeat,
sometimes it is
victory.

There are moments when I forget that my heart is held together with duct tape. Recently I had one of those mornings…

I Forgot

As my eyes opened to the day
I dreamt of life away
And, I forgot
As the sun came into view
Before, I thought of you,
I forgot
My dog snuggled at my feet,
She gazed at me so, sweet
And, I forgot
Taking a clean deep breath
No thought of life or death
I forgot
Experiencing peace, love and grace
A smile briefly creased my face
When, I forgot
Now, I write about the feeling
Of a life that was not reeling
When, I forgot

I have to be ready to let go

I have to be ready to let go
To realize I have all I want

I have to be willing to give up
To find my freedom to choose

I have to unchain my heart
To find it was never tethered

I have to trust my own voice
To hear the deeper things of God and life

I have to write a love letter
To understand that I am loved

I have to be willing to forgive
To find peace

I have to look at me without shame
To accept unconditional love

I have to do all and nothing
To find myself among the debris of my self-condemnation

I have to love what I discover
To live, love and be me.

So They Say No

No you're not enough
Is often spoken
Without words
By rolling eyes
Head turned
Face stony
No
Is a glance
Towards another
Shaking the head
Tsk tsk
No
Can be a killer of dreams
A stab in the gut
A questioning of one's worth
Rejection
No
Can stop you in your tracks
When accepted as truth
Can suck up your joy
Who you?
No
The voice of another's not you
    You're a girl
    You're too young too old
    You're not talented enough

You're too... anything or not
Enough of something
If you listen
You're paralyzed
Noes echoing in the darkness
Of the now self-imposed
Prison of needing approval
Spread your arms
See the walls fall
The light rush in
With a resounding yes
I am all I need
Ever be
I am me and I'm
Good enough
Step out
Released of the need to
Care about what others'
    Opinions
    Judgments
    Jealousies
    Self-righteousness
    Know it all-ness
    Fear
    Intimidation
    Self-importance
    Status quo requirements are
To Look deep

Within for what you know to be true
It's really great to be you
The one and only
Unique you and you
Are all you need to be
Be
Being
True to your calling
Without anyone else
Agreeing
Give yourself permission
To just be
In celebration of the gift
That is you
Say yes.
Leaving the buts behind
Say yes
And don't look back
The only no you need
Is to say no to noes
You're not...
Stop right there
I am more than enough
I'm saying yes to all that
Life has to offer

My Time is My Own?

It's late
No matter
I'm just beginning
To realize
My life is my own
The voice that says
Do this…no that
Has no power any longer

The rise of guilt into my throat
Bile of days gone by
People with power over me
Don't exist
It's difficult to realize
My time is my own

So many years focused
Upon achievement
Making a difference
Leading the charge
Finding the answers
Solving the problem
Putting out the fire

I never really asked the questions
Is all this doing… mine
Are these choices answers

To questions I never asked
I stay up too late
Dishes in the sink
Go to the beach
Buy a silly hat
And the only one wagging
Their finger at me is me

God won't love me more or less
If I sit on the floor playing LEGOs
Or raise money for charity
Love isn't based on what I do
Except the love from me
Now that love is conditional

Constant reminder
Listen
Live
Love
With grace doing onto
Others has become
Give self the
Compassion
I give to you

I'm going to sit with myself
Let go of judging
Criticizing
And belittling me

Freed from the prison
Of my own creation
I'll do the dishes in the morning

The Path to Truth

The path to truth
Isn't always clear
Obstacle free
Or without peril
The path to truth
Doesn't always reveal
What's on the other side
Reaching the destination
Can be difficult
    Rocky
    Slippery
    Treacherous
The path to truth
Is always
Worth the effort
Scraped knees
Stretched muscles
Fear of the unknown
The path to truth
Is the journey
Of determined honesty
Against lies and deceit
Representative of empathy
And compassion
For those in the cross hairs
Of mouths that defame
Be not afraid to walk
The path to Truth

Pure LOVE

Pure love doesn't
emanate in the mind,
it can't be conjured up
bought in a department store
won by a stroke of luck
or wished for on a birthday

Pure love was with us
when we entered the world
and greets us when we exit

Pure love is ours to give away
as we pass through the lives of others
sharing this amazing planet

Through giving love
we are constantly refilled

Want more love
give more away

Perfection

*In my years of shame from failure, I didn't always learn new lessons,
I piled on to the shame of the old. I suppose that is the lesson learned.
I now know the cause and effect of piling on — deteriorated health
and wellness.
Broken hearts and relationships.*

*Now I give myself permission to not be perfect.
Perfection was a requirement in my childhood either from my
family or perhaps, myself.
If I was only perfect, then I would be loved. Conditionally.*

*Leaping into my future without the constraints of perfection.
Learning to love my self and others without (so many) conditions.
Not being perfect, I still recognize my intolerances and judgments.
I also realize that in writing about love I don't have to have perfect
love.
I have the choice of practicing loving kindness, every day.
Being love, lovable and loving, not striving for it, is something I can
write about.*

Saying Yes

Are there times
Fear rules and
We say no to life's
Opportunities
Experiences
Challenges
No to
Stretching
Reaching for our highest potential
Exercising our leadership
Allowing the idea of failure
Or fear of success
To paralyze
Cripple
Contain
Our will
Leaving us
Floating in a windless sea
Allowing waves to batter
Pushing us off course
By abdicating our power
Or choosing not to choose
A direction
A lost ship
Unknown navigational tools
Drifting into oblivion

No idea what port
Is home
If lucky
Not crashing upon the rocks
Initiating a course
Making a purposeful
Decision
Assembling the resources
Daring fate
Grabbing the wheel
Taking the helm
Reaching for the North Star
Testing the winds
Setting our own sail
Dumping excess baggage
Letting go of
Worrying of what others
Are thinking of us
Taking on the challenge
No matter what the outcome
Knowing that courses
Can be adjusted
Maybe this wasn't about
Winning
Or losing
Success
or failure
Perhaps it was the moment

We accepted we could lead
Our self
Be our own hero
Take responsibility
To sail
Into the unknown
Under our own flag
Saying a profound
Yes to life's
Opportunities
Experiences
Exercises in leadership
It could just be finding
Yes
In the port
Worth discovering

Keepin' the lights a Burnin'

Awake at three
How often will this
Opportunity
Present itself
To enjoy the tree
In quiet with
Just me
I love the Light
The reflections of what
Could be
I treasure the memories
Celebrating
A birthing
Of hope
We all need hope
The story of unwed
Mother
Border Crossings
Escaping tyranny
Humble beginnings
What good can come from Galilee
No casting stones
Bring me the children
Share the fish
Give the bread
Trust he said

Love is the answer
Most important of all
Most important of all
Love
Remember the Light
Hanukkah
Celebrate the Light
Solstice
Honor the Light
Sing the songs
Be kind
Grateful
Giving
Do no harm
Not in word or deed
Up at three
With just me and the tree
Celebrating the Lights
Remembering

Layers

I write. I write all the time. rambling, musing, listening to the voice and words, I write.

Today, I'm thinking and writing about the layers of guilt, anger, stories, regrets, labels, self judgment, worries and expectations we are covered with—like a homeless lady in her many layers of clothes. We may be afraid to give any of them up. Letting fear of who we may discover, cause us to keep piling on more layers until the real person inside is nearly invisible. Even though we are exhausted with the weight and heat of carrying all of this around non-stop – we are more afraid of who we will find if we give up that shell of persona protection we have wrapped ourselves in.

Overcoming the fear to peel away each layer may be difficult yet, necessary to get to the truth of who we are meant to be. Letting go of the worn-out outer garments to find the love that resides inside. Learning to accept and begin to see yourself in a new way as worthy of love and giving love. Worthy of creating a life worth the living – if we would only shed those many layers to find the naked truth of our own light and beauty.

What a glorious day to shed all the excess weight and be free.

Some Thoughts on Thinking and Truth

Thinking thoughts through
Tempted to believe

Yet, thoughts are just mulling
Stressing, supposing, surmising
Affected by history and memory
Thoughts are
Not necessarily truth
Paraphrasing the Katie Byron questions
Is it truth? Are you sure it's true?
How do you know?
Can the answer come from thinking?

Thoughts can be internal
Judgment, gossip,
About self or other
critical or ideological
What are thoughts made of?

They're really just electro-chemical
reactions, scientists tell us
The number and complexity
Make them hard to fully understand.

Basically we are soul filled living computers
Thinking is based on what data we've

On our DNA operating system
Added to our hard drive and the apps we've downloaded

Some of us think about stuff more than others.
There are days when I have to turn off my operating system
Meditation helps
Just breathing deeply and allowing
Thoughts to float on through
I say thanks for stopping by
But I don't invite them in for tea
Sleep is great until I wake up
Technicolor movie in progress
Right now
I'm going to stop thinking of thinking
What was that?

Every heart has a story

Every heart has a story
To be told
Every life has a role
To be played
Every person has a purpose
To be expressed
Written
Danced
Not bottled up
Afraid of what others
May think
Held back by a sense of unworthiness
Battered by other's opinions
Waiting for permission
Too busy to listen to our-self
Tomorrow I'll take time to be me
Every day that is put off
The story grows colder
Fingers stiffer
Heart stonier
Mind wandering
What was that life
I used to hear calling
The one I shoved away
Until the drum-beat grew dimmer
Sun lost its shimmer

Forgotten is the one
Precious life I meant to live

Finding Life In The midst of Loss

Full of funerals

Lately, my life has been full of funerals. When I was younger it was full of weddings, baby showers, pot lucks, BBQs, work events, concerts, sports and graduations. Now, it's the retirement parties, memorials of lives spent, not beginning. And yet the birthings are still there.

In my re-wirement I'm fortunate enough to have the time to learn, reflect, be in nature, meditate and pray. I've found more of me, developed a deeper understanding of love, I have friends who don't try to slip me into old uncomfortable boxes. I can break away from perhaps self-imposed confinement and try on new ideas and ways of being.

I've found acceptance in this time of life without constantly having to explain why I thought or believed as I did 30 years ago. Others my age also appreciate this freedom from expectations, regret and my own and other's opinions of who or what I was.

So, while I'm going to all these funerals. I'm learning so much more about people. We've all been many things in this life, had good and not so good relationships with others. We've accomplished and failed and no one person really knows the whole story except the person who passed on, and they're not telling.

Until we finally shut our eyes – life isn't finished with us yet.

The Living Tombstone

The greatness of love is it's unending, expanding nature.

The more you experience unconditional love in your life—the more your heart expands to capture even more, sharing it back out into the world.

A heart of love never shrinks from adding to its girth. With each breath and life affirming moment, love grows.

Losing a loved one doesn't mean we need to become a living tombstone to their memory. Loving others never diminishes the love you had, it purely affirms the goodness that was and is true love.

I've had losses and some broken relationships, yet the God who is love, my joyous friends, close family, and the loving man who makes life beautiful, have warmed and expanded my heart to new dimensions. Love is not static, it's ever expanding, and knows no boundaries.

Life may change but love remains.

Facing Death

Facing death
Your own
Or one's loved
Is more about
Looking straight on
At life

I have an image.
Of being met
With open arms
Laughter and love
Job done
Gauntlet run
Is it true
Could it be so
That we're on assignment
Deployed for a time
Birth to death
Our commitment
Our service time
Boot camp
The life lived
Our learning to love
Class over
Then everybody dies
    Born
    Middle

Die
It's life in the middle
What am I learning
What truly matters
Be kind
Don't lie
Love and listen
Take action against
Rage
Greed
Hate
Change the rigid
Thinking yes my own
Don't waste the life given
On resentment or judgments
Trying to make right
The perceived wrongs
According to your own
Way of thinking
Who gives more
Who does less
There will always be self
Involved people who do not
Value the gifting in others
Energy drains
Understand the difference
In giving taking receiving
You know you can feel it
Deeply in your soul

She Wrote her Death in her Life

Inspired by the poetry of Sylvia Plath

The words we read
The notes we jot
The poems we absorb
The passages sought

Sylvia Plath
"Dying is an art…"

Her words pound
Deeply into my heart
More than foreshadowing
She toyed with death as
She wrote her life

As I read my breath quickens
Did people not see
Or was her pathos
so brilliant
They shielded their eyes

One year later gone
Mother of two
This attempt successful
She'd fulfilled her art
Masterpiece done

Words cannot be ignored
She expressed them so well
Raw
Bone crunching
She looked to complete her opus

No Names to Mark the Days

There are no names to mark the days
When hospice care lives in your home
Only another morning when light displaces darkness
The breaths come more slowly
As if time itself slows
Listening intently
As with a newly birthed child
For each measured breath
Hospice nurse says it's near
You whisper in the ear
Oh how much I love you
Then it
Stops
The breath
The day
The life
Seeped away

Never the Same

Just yesterday I was grateful
Today I don't like me
I slip
Into old discomforts
My head aches
My hip shouts
I need to shower but I want to lie about
Anxious for a future
I cannot see
What in the world is happening
To me
This human experience
Is sometimes bizarre
My life in the shadows
Or in a glass jar
Emotions ride the angry
Roller coaster or
Easily glide by
On the merry
Go round
Get out
Go ahead
Move
I scream in silence
I know I know
The pine air is so healing

The gnats not so appealing
Always a price
Ebb and flow of life
Yesterday was flow
Today I'm ebbing away.

These words were written in response to mass murder, shootings and children being taken at the borders and the pervasive fear that rocks our nation.

Speechless

Speechless
No need to offend
Defend
Pretend
I can not comprehend
I'm bereft of words
To explain
The loss, the pain
The rift in humanity
This senseless calamity
An act of insanity
Horrific beyond belief
Causing nothing but grief
While my pen scribbles
My mind tries to understand
And I'm
Speechless

32 seconds – 9 dead

So many of my poems deal with love and death. Writing helps me handle the devastation. I was writing today of the unconscionable deaths by assault weapons, how quickly they can take lives – 32 seconds and 9 dead. I looked at memories. Last year I wrote:

A poem is forming
Written excuse
Penned hall pass
Scribbled emotions
My way of processing
What living
Is passing
Into dying
When death is
Crawling away
With yet another soul
Souls
I'm not ready
Are we ever
Breathe into the words
One more family with loss
Impossible to imagine
Only the words can
Speak cold truth
Inevitable truth
All that live

Will pass
But who has the right
To steal a life

Have I Expired?

If every day is new
and now is all we have
Is it ever too late
For a new beginning?
Is there a "use by date"
attached to life?
Each time I finish a project
I start thinking it's my last one
then, wham!
A new idea pops up.
I'm thinking that the "use by date"
Isn't up until life is.

Sunday thinking on a Saturday

Have you made a "Bucket List"
for living, not for dying?
You know, the list
All those things you really
Believe you are
Had hoped to be or do
Yet, you keep deciding
You don't have the money
Others need you too much
Better to lose ten pounds
You don't deserve
To take the time
Spend the money
It isn't the safe
Approved
Cautious thing to do?
Are you waiting
Until a terrible diagnosis

The kids are all OK

Your parents are well cared for

The job is finally done

House is paid off
To finally say, it's all right

Go ahead do or be your one delicious self
What if you wait too long?
If you aren't living out your
Bucket List, now
It's time to question
Your "whys"
Let go
Of what others
Even you
Think of yourself
Once that decision
Is made to just be yourself
Imperfect with warts and all
Watch how many doors open
For those experiences to
Be checked off your list
You are open to the adventure
Of more things to add
Some you never dreamed
Were possible
The biggest surprise
Those people you worried about
Are all too busy
With their own life to be concerned
About who you are
What you did or didn't do
The kids are OK
The parents are well enough

The job gets done

And maybe the house isn't
paid for but it turns out
you didn't want
to live there anyway.

Even though I quit working at supporting other creatives as a fulltime effort and now – I'm not who I used ta' be, there is a lot more yet in me.

The end of the used ta' be tour or is it?

When young I didn't realize
How quickly age could creep
Blindsided.
Now firmly in its grasp
Invisible
Inconsequential
Indefensible
Eyes of youth glancing past

What value the antiquated
Exhibited, used ta' be a somebody

Like Rilke's Panther circling
Caged
From without and within
No longer able to see the forest
Fire of freedom
To be eventually quenched
Lie down, quit pacing, find rest

No.
What they
The they of them

Don't get
Realize
Comprehend
If I close my eyes to life's joy, creating
That would be my end

When Silence is Cruel

Silence
A lethal weapon
Shook in the face
Of understanding
Brings death
To relationship
Silence
The punisher
Leaves you all alone
Refusal to engage
An impasse impossible
To bridge
Silence can be golden
Or the cruelest form
Of communication

Hard to see in the chill of loss

In the chill of loss
Or fear of loss
It's hard to find the blessings
Tears flowing
Veiling our sight
Frozen fast to cheek
What if like the rainbow
after the raging storm
Colorful hope comes
Shining the light of understanding
Through our watery fears
Look there
Our blessings are there
As tearful yearnings dry
Frozen surface melts
Revealing what was hidden
Come closer
Here
The blessings of newness are here
We just hadn't seen them yet

The Caged Heart

I was in a marriage, married twice to the same man, it was a difficult, loveless, combative time. I felt I failed to be a wife, and mother, and I had failed God. The second time, I finally realized if I wanted to live I had to escape the cage of judgment I had built for myself. I wrote this within days of the separation.

Releasing the heart
From the cage of life gone wrong
Love swept away, gone
Paralyzed, no movement at all
Keys rattling, door slowly opens

Looking around at the perch
And wires where I could see
But, dared not venture
What was I thinking, fear cries out
Maybe, my cage wasn't so bad

It was a mess, unfinished
Stepping over stuff to find myself
Caged in the mire,
Couldn't breathe, heart broken
Yet familiar, please help me

No, reverberated from the wires

I see the sky, sparkling light
Break free, fly from what I know
To the possibility of what could be
Is it safe out there
Will I find the freedom to choose

Unfamiliar territory; freedom

Don't know how this story will end
No need for approval, or blame
Not asking for acceptance, or agreement
Stretching my wings, feeling the call to home
Here I am
Into the unknown I fly

Tick Tock

Ten days
Forty seven years
Two hours
Tomorrow
Right now
Life is counted
By the minutes
Ticking by on a clock
Commemorated
Celebrated
Bemoaned
Or
Regretted
Time doesn't care
Only we define
How we think of
Our calculations of time
We are told not to waste
Time
Can you ever actually
Waste what is yours to spend
Freely
But that fits with there's only
So much time in a day
In a life – a bank account of sorts
If I spend 10 days sitting bedside

Is it wasted
It's gone but
Never wasted
When used with love

As the sun rises

The sun is rising
With it the clouds
Become visible
The dewy trees shine
What wasn't visible
Becomes brightly lit

Bring on the light
Shine in on the hidden
Fearful darkness
Of the unknown
Warm the frozen surface
Of secrets held tightly

Eyes blink back tears
Of missing what was
Heart opens to newness
Letting go of it's always been
To see what can be
What is – is up to me

Scent matters

Scent matters
Pine
Melted candles
Wood fire
Baking bread
Stew stewing
Salty ocean mists
River washing rocks
Warm winds blowing
Old wood library
Books opening

Nursing homes
Could benefit from
Smell therapy
Filled with flowers
Breath of new borns
And puppies too
Cinnamon cider
Rosemary
Lilac and lavender
Aromas of hope and
Happier days when bodies
Worked
Legs and arms
Took flight
Scents that transcend
The entrapment of bed

Retired Rewired Reworked

Walked away
Willingly from
The paycheck
What's next
Income slashed
Don't care
Or really care
For self
For life
For creation
For finishing up what was started
At birth
Struggled with in the middle
With the end creeping
Ever closer
If not now
Will I die with my story
Untold
Does anyone want to know
Do I
Maybe my story is just
For me and maybe it's
Also for you
So here I sit
Retired
Rewired

Reworked
To create my own
Ending to my story
Maybe to encourage you
What's your story
How do you tell it
Is it danced, written, sketched
Hoping it's loved
I'm thinking there's a lot
More living
In the last years of dying

Google what?

At my Mom's helping her get her house ready for a family visit in honor of my sister and brother in law's anniversary. My 85 year old Mom, just walked into the kitchen, she looked at me a bit confused.

"I think my rememberer is broken, I don't know why I came in here." She laughed as she started to wander off.

I told her: Don't feel bad Mom, my rememberer is keeping yours company, do they have a fix it shop for that?

Where did we put the phone book? Do we have one? I can Google it! I jokingly said. "Google what?" She asked.

Love the memories of not remembering.

I may be done

I may be done
Or I may not be at all
If I be
Will I do
If I do
Am I being
So much to consider
The being
The doing
The staying
The going
What if I'm done
And I'm just hanging around
Am I still being
Is there purpose
Yet to be
I write because I hear
I hear the words
If I hear must I write
Are wordings beings
Or doings
No thought of my own
Forms upon my lips
I'm hiding from my own
Resentments
Disappointments

Judgments
Lack of purpose
It's one of those days
Had I painted
It would be in the fire
It's a what's it all
About kinda day
I may be done
Or just begun
By letting go of expectations
Expectant of even more
Molten lava hitting ice
Hardens into stone
I'm hardened
Steam rising
Hissing is all I hear
Is that exhalation
The breath in
Held at bay
It's usually after
The long expiring breath outward
That new life sucks in
Hopeful creativity comes rushing
Filling the emptiness
Thoughts of I'm done
Are washed away
The ebb turns to flow
I'm waiting

Today
The ebb seems longer
The flow slower
The enough isn't
Satisfying the need
Of inspirational
Joy
My belly ache is real
But the lack of feeling in
My gut is more concerning
Or more calming
Is this how I'd spend my last day
Waiting
Silently listening
at the train station
For the whistle to blow

satirical nonsense, no belly ache remedies needed.

Belly Aching

Some days when your belly aches
And you have so much to do
You wonder why
Does this have to happen to you
Why is the vessel that carries you breaking down in mid stream
What did you do to it
For it to treat you so mean

What is the disconnect with duties, deadlines and the weakness
in your bowels
Why does the mind say go and the body says sit down

While frustration fills your mouth with bile
It looks like you'll be here for awhile

Love yourself, love your body, ha!

Right now you'd like to disconnect
Keep moving on to complete the tasks
let the body go ahead – take a rest
What possible purpose is there for you to interfere
You have no time to deal with this – what a pain in the rear
The IRS doesn't care that you're not well
You can't cross a border until your passport is fulfilled
Money doesn't go in banks unless you take it to…

The constant rumbling in your belly
Keeps you staring blankly at the telly
Stupid rhymes
won't make up for fines
For not getting things done on time
While you lie awake in bed
Shaking your still sadly attached head
Belly aching about the belly ache
Is there no app for this? SIRI?

The years I cried in silence

I just read my journals of
Trying to survive
The living in
The midst of the dying

Losses
Security
Who I thought I was
What I believed my life to be
Love was going to leave
Feeling I'd never know it again
I wrote
I wrote a lot with grave
Blank days interspersed
By silence when my voice
Written or spoken was dead

Always the cheerful one
Cook
Beautiful meals change everything
If I can't take away the truth of cancer
I can cook
I can eat
We can all enjoy dinner
Isn't this good

I staved off
Fear anger sorrow
By writing
My worries of
Aloneness
could I survive
Who would I be
If not the wife, caretaker,
Mother — would my
Identity be intact

No
I was not intact
I was broken
Shattered holding on
To a thin veneer of hope
Plan
Look forward to something
Anything
Diversion
Distraction push back
Depression

Sitting staring into darkness
Friends would prod the coals
Trying to ignite the flame of my life
The world kept turning
As people flew off into the void
And yet I held on

Why I kept asking
I'm too tired to keep trying
It takes a lot of effort to live
Take me I bargained
God wasn't in a bargaining mood

Exhausted
Trying to maintain
Some semblance of
Normality
Nurturing
Natural order
Any kind of order
In the face of emergency rooms
Infusion chairs
Chemo brain confusion
Anger as he got more
And more frightened at losing control
Yet love grew
Acceptance
Laughter
Tenderness
Gratefulness for what we had
Where we'd been
Mixed with tears of what
We were never going to be again
As care taker and passer
We did and did and did
Until there was no more

Doing to be done.
Only farewell
Not separated by choice
But we were both exhausted
Hands slipped apart
and under the water of death
He went

There's Light in Me Yet

Stepping into the
Morning as black
Transformed to blue
One star in the sky
Bravely stated
I'm not done
There's light in me
Yet
Don't give up
Keep shining
Keep hoping
Keep keeping
The light
Burning

The Tides of the Creative Soul

Words

Learning to read at a very early age I discovered that words have immense power to evoke an emotion, set a course, spark imagination and offer an alternative life where there was pain or sadness.

Words.

I didn't know these truths at age eight, I just knew to my core that reading opened the doors to my mind and I would walk through and be each character or pick one that I wanted to emulate.

Words.

I escaped into words. By ten I had traveled the Far East with Pearl S. Buck. Traveled to Hawaii and lived at Tara during the Civil War. Stories of England, Russia and Ireland would have earned me frequent flyer miles.

Words.

My absolute joy of the written word comes from being transported from reality into fantasy or an alternative state of reality.

Write Write Write

A few thoughts after a day of writing: I write because I read. I read sides of boxes, scribbles on walls, (including FB) pamphlets to trilogies. Every few months, or years I even read some of my own writing. The multiple journals that stuff boxes; once written upon now cast aside. Grabbing for the next empty canvas to fill – I keep writing. Pretty floral covered or college lined student notebooks, any paper will do. My family saved the scraps of writings from dry cleaner receipts written on while in parking lots. If my handwriting is on it, they tuck it away somewhere in an envelope of similar writings.

Some are my nonsensical whimseys, some opinions, plans for an event or retreat, imagined hurts, real pain and joys and every once in a while an inspired nugget that stops me cold and demands a re-read. Who wrote that with my hand, I question.

I know that when I hear write, write, write, something is coming that I should pay attention to – something that after I write it down, that I then read myself for the first time.

The thing is dear friends, if I wasn't already writing I would never hear "write" three times and I would never be privy to the words that were going to flow from my pen.

Strangely, I fight the writing, painting or other creative pursuit…I have to make an appointment and set a deadline to do the very things I love. Perversity at its best, self sabotage?

Maybe, maybe I'm just afraid that today my muse, my inspiration, the Spirit that fills me with wisdom beyond my comprehension won't show up. But, if I don't pick up the pen it's a for sure thing, nothing will happen.

Aha moments

I love aha moments
Poetry that captures my breath
Silences my thoughts
Time suspended for an instant
sunrises
sunsets
trees
water
Stepping across the threshold
ancient building
place of worship
art museum
bookstore or library
Breathing in all the breaths of those before me
Surrounded by all forms of creativity
Literary
Visual
Musical
Performing Art
Give my curious mind
Conversation
Social discourse
Civil debate
Interaction with thinking beings
All ahas that make me think and ponder

Culinary Arts

I propose that food, especially really good food is an installation art form. As an artist I am a sensory person. Poetry resonates in my soul, music moves my heart; art works of all forms capture my attention and admiration.

Gastronomical delights are equally savored, each morsel is given proper attention. For me preparing or eating a lovely meal or drinking fine wines is a creative encounter.

Creative Inspiration

In spirit
Being inspired
Inspiring others
Creativity is inspiration in action
Taking form
Evoking emotion
Encouraging critical thinking
Breathing life
One of the greatest joys
Being an inspiration
One of the greatest gifts
Receiving inspiration
Inspire each other
Fan the flames
Coax life
Dig deep
Deeper still
Create from your heart and soul
Do all things with love
Infuse spirit
Create
Dance
Share
Write
Sing
Art

Love for the Arts

I love the arts for all the unexplainable reasons
I am in love with the creative process
The way the arts give meaning to my existence.

Love
For the beauty of the line drawn on the canvas
Spoken on the stage
Unable to look away
I am a changed person.

Love
The encounter with a few words
So powerfully blended in a sentence
Poem, or song that they hold my breath hostage
Let me hear that again.

Love
I am drawn into the perfectly composed sonata
Guitar solo, photograph, or footfall of the dancer
I know the joy
I respect the hours of dedicated practice
it takes to achieve that
    One moment
    Note
    Perfect shot
Beautiful choreography.

These things are sometimes unexplainable
To those who do not share that love
I no longer try to explain the mysterious
Joy that wells up
Like my spiritual walk
My creative nature
My love for trees, sunsets and water
All rises up from the depth of my soul and cries out for more.

In a Paradise Lost

Let kindness
Greet the day
Grateful for the breath
The ability to express
Our truth
As did a young
Picasso in 1901
Along with
Others of his generation
Proclaimed the world
A paradise lost
Yet, we know it's
Just in the process
Of being found
Often wrought with
Tears
Fears
Sear-ing
Pain
I offer you hope
As he offered us
Child With a Dove
Out of centuries old
Struggle
Partisanship
Them against us

Us against them
Starvation of body and soul
The artists and poets
Proclaim still
Peace
Held close and tenderly
In the arms of a child
The palette, colors, words
We pass on
To the newest
Observers
Empathetic story tellers
Yet to come
Hope
Peace
Kindness
Sung
Written
Created
In a paradise lost
Waiting to be found

Words fall from the sky

Write, and write again, keep writing until the neural pathway is rutted into your brain like the chariot wheels into the hard rock surface of Pompeii. Then writing becomes the writer, it's who you are.

At night words
fall from the sky,
shooting stars searing my mind
sparking my imagination
I see them
In the morning
they rise from the earth
evaporating mists floating
upwards into oblivion
I hear them
calling

in the sunrise and sunset
their presence is most felt
the crescendo
falling meets the rising
the light is most impactful
they dare me
capture my meaning
if you can
write
keep up

ah, there goes one
what was that
I felt it go through
my soul
I saw it briefly
yet it escaped
my pen
leaving behind
the knowing of its existence
taunting me to bring it back
ember dying in the crash to earth
futility to hold the mist in my grasp
I write on
waiting for the next meteoric shower
with my butterfly net
and mason jar

Poetically thinking

In awe of Toi Derracotte

Every word is a poem prompt
I speak in poetry cadence
I jot down a phrase
I awake from a sleep I haven't slept
That's a title
Toi's voice
Reverberates
Grab my phone
Write in notes
Remember the joy of before
Surviving
Escaping
Enduring
the middle
Climbing out
New middles
Another middle
Living with the remnants
Sorrowful
Cleansing
Sobs
Letting go
Joy in the after
There may be

More middles
Damn
Oh oh oh oh oh oh floats through
Only some will know
It's in their wildest dreams

And this is me

There is this
And this is me
Then there is that
And it's also me

One above in
the clouds you see
One below
Amongst the trees

Above
Wind and clouds
Beckon and greet me
Below
Squirrels and birds
Constantly entreat me

There is this
And this is me
Then there is that
And it's also me

A creative's space
In either place
Come
Art with me
Above or below the trees

The Irish Experience

When curiosity
Far exceeds
  Fear of the unknown
  Complacency
  Comfort zones
The body travels
  Mind expands
  Spirit soars
  Soul is enriched
An Irish experience
  Enhances my life
  Enlarges my heart
  Broadens my views

Testing my Muse

On vacation expecting to write. A week has passed – no poem has formed
A silly ditty comes from trying to force feed a poem before I leave!

Get quiet
Go sit on the deck
The geese claim my attention
They honk and peck
Announcing their arrival
Ending their long mating trek
They preen, pose and arch
Their beautiful long neck

Pick me,
Pick me
Their intent, I suspect

My inner critic cries
"What the heck"
I talk back,
"Just give me a sec
I'm writing long hand,
Not using high tech"
Nothing is coming,
My mind's a train wreck

The muse says
"Give me your attention
What did you expect
You ask for a poem,
Where is my respect"
Sorry, I sigh…
But it has no effect

I give up
Back to the geese
Proudly stretching their neck
I'll write another day
When there's time to reflect

Metaphorically speaking

It appears
That everything in my life is a metaphor
An analogy
A way of thinking
I see word upon word
In poems
In the red zone – a title
Skin. Trees. Wind
Colors. Clouds. Hands
Yes, even Words
Everything and everybody
Has a story to tell
A rock reminds me of a journey
A journey reminds me of a life
A life reminds me of a path
The path leads me to love
Love
Well, I could write a poem about that!

No Black or White

I write
Then I fight
With wrong and right
For there is no black or white
Dark gray to light
Marbled sight
I write

Coffee with Mary

I look in
And he sleeps
While sleeping there is no pain
Coffee in hand
Mary Oliver to keep me company
I sit
Head shaking at
The beauty of her words
Loneliness disappears
Mary is here
I look in again
And still he sleeps
It's a different kind of loneliness
It's a missing of what was
Robust laugh
Tinged now with pain and worry
Mary says: "Oh Lord how shining and festive
is your gift to us, if only we look and see."
I look in again
Grateful that still he sleeps
This gift's enough

Dear Agatha

How could you leave
Where are the clever
Mysteries without salaciousness
Horror not required
I miss
Hercule and Miss Marple
Mysteries
Oh how I love a mystery
Make me reason
Growing up with Nancy Drew
Sherlock and Watson too
Where's the fun
Of Asta and the Thin Man
Or the search for a falcon
Then in my eleventh year
Mom started handing
Me Agatha's intrigues
Never telling me the ending but
Always asking: where are you now?
Smiling she'd say: Oh, just wait.
How could I?
Pulling out the flashlight
I roamed English country sides
From under my blanket
I searched for clues
The butler is too obvious

Just one more chapter
Please?
By the time I was 15
I'd watched so many English movies on PBS
That I had the accidental accent
Still do, I gather as
I'm asked where in England
I'm from.
The San Francisco region
I reply Yes
Where the fog rolls in
And my apparent accent with it.
Voice rising at the end of the sentence
Not intentionally
First time in England I felt right at home
Went to Baker Street to visit Sherlock
Sat in the pubs
And visited the villages seeing
The mysteries unfold.
Awe, Agatha there's just
No equal to you.
I've read these books until
The jacket covers are ripped and gone
Where's my tea
I'm sure a blanket's near by
And Then There Were None

Birthing Poetry

Just so you know
Some poems are birthed
Ever so easily
Breathe
Whew whew whew
Here she comes
It's love at first sight

Others
Long labor
Pain
Pain
More
Hours of yelling
Ugly words
Forcing the poem to life
Exhausted
It's love at second or third sight

In Honor of an Artist Friend

Without seeing, I hear
A gentleness
In his soul
A sweetness of spirit
Tempered by experience
Refined in the fire
A man of nature
With inner strength
He captures the essence of life
He sees the world with
Eyes that seek to know
Not just observe yet
Observe he does
While reaching inside
To that place of knowing
Not enough to just glance
Deeper he goes, let me in
I hear him say in the silent breath of time
See me in my art
See my heart in my creations
I am one with the voice of all

I write what I need to hear. A couple years ago I wrote this.

Revelation

When revelation
and innovation knock
on the door of stagnation
and status quo,
invite them in.
Great things can happen
if you let go of old
expectations and ways
of doing things
to try on
new ways.
Thinking
Relating
Creating
Seeing
Being

Came across these words from 2015 while gathering my poems and writings together. I'm ready. Now is the time. Those dripping words have found a home.

My El Niño Year

Words are dripping from my fingers
Flooding the paper
Notions, thoughts, inspirations
Heart and soul bursting forth
Life spilled out in an inky sacrifice
All for the muse of writing
Like rain upon the parched lands
This just may be my El Niño year

Haiku Times 2

I love the cryptic
Flow of words for you to guess
The meaning hidden

God no God nature
Spins webs tells stories leaving
Us searching for truth

Worth Knowing

Nothing truly worth knowing
Can be fully explained
We just don't have the capacity
To explain the unexplainable
To understand eternity with
Fleeting thoughts
The best we can do
Is create symbols
Words strung together in poetry
Tell the stories of acts and adventures
Heaven and Hell that dwells within
Expressively created art
Musical melodies attempting
The revelation of knowing
The unknowable

In the Heart of the Poet

In the heart of the poet
Time stops
The breath of inspiration
Blows out the pretenses
Strips naked the soul
Senses are heightened
The trees are greener
The sun brighter
Sounds – well, noisier
Silence deeper
Surface layers are peeled away
Until creation is birthed
In the heart of the poet

Acknowledgements

With Gratitude

Birthing poetry is not for the faint of heart. It takes a team of supporters, guides and encouragers to birth the thoughts and musings into creation.

Grateful for family, friends, fellow writers, and creatives, who encouraged and yes, who helped me push through the pain of transition in my life and kept saying you're not done yet…when I wanted to quit. They are the reason this collection was published.

In Poetry and Photography with Friends, the words are my compositions with contributions by my Facebook friends, some I've never met in person before—yet, we are in a wonderful way, old style pen pals. Words and images have drawn us together. Words and images are what this book is comprised of to bring you this poetic life's journey. Debi Benson Bradford graciously presents her enchanting ocean photography to draw you into the powerfully calm waters.

Divine intervention, serendipity, or the luck of the Irish, introduced me to author, artist Mary Anne Radmacher, this book's birthing coach and she to Barbara Grassey, the Book Boss, who acted as the midwife to be sure that birthing had a healthy and beautiful beginning to life.

Judith Cassis lent her expertise as a New York and LA times best selling ghost writer and writing teacher. She, in her gentle way, kept inviting me to write, publishing my articles in her writer's books.

My sons Carlin Jones and Christopher Parks, along with my husband, other family members and friends who should be family, kept telling me, you have something to say. Say it. Do this.

Many creative women inspired me, teaching me to stretch – Bo Mackinson, Carol Gage Andrews, Sue Deininger, Debi Benson Bradford, Jill Davis, Pam Matchie Thiede, and Shirley Brewer are but a few of the cadre of stars that shine in my sky.

Last but never least, My Mother, who gave me birth, kept every word I'd ever written. I had tossed years of writings into cardboard boxes after a very painful divorce and swore off most everything I believed in, including my writing. My Mom saved them all. During my late husband Nelson's six year battle with cancer, I started to journal again. Mom, pleased to see I was writing again, informed me she had kept all the old writings and had read some of them—her instructions: Do not throw them away. With her encouragement I wrote more. I cried and wrote. I laughed and wrote. I listened and wrote inspirations I heard in the star dust. She encouraged me to tell my story. The memoir of life with love and cancer was published eight years ago. She loved me to read her my poetry as she struggled in her last years of life. Momma I am forever, grateful.

Special Acknowledgement for Poetry with Friends

Some gave a word, others a line. All are appreciated.

Caren Albers
Carol Gage Andrews
Dena Barskin
Connie Bennett
Toni Wikswo Best
Ilena Bortolin-Sternberg
Debi Benson Bradford
Shirley Brewer
Jill Davis
David Dowdy
Cindy Galt
Susie Werner Geiger
Janell Genoud
LeonorLi Matthews Gibbs
Pamela Giumarra
Janet Hudson
Miriam M. Hughes
Kate Lalor
Sandra Pieper Larson
Debbie Lowe
Bo Mackison
Sharon Martinelli
Bill McCutchen
Deanna Nelson

Margie Stewart Noriega
Norene Polack
Susan Reep
Annabella Rusen
Ruth Smith
Wynnde Sue
Shelley Surratt
Janet Sutton
Carole Swanston

About the Author

Jeanette Richardson Herring is an artist who expresses herself in multi media, including storytelling and musing. Communicating through memoir, prose, and poetry are some of the ways she tells her stories. Her arts career has provided opportunities to share her love of life in art galleries and museums, events, publications, radio and television. As a thinker, dreamer and encourager, supporting and advocating for artists for many years, she has worked in many creative capacities including as ED for an Arts Council. While continuing to coach and give workshops for non profits, cities, universities and arts organizations, she is happiest among the trees of Pine Mountain Club, with her sweetheart, family and friends – enjoying life creating literary and visual arts. You may contact her at Jeanette@PineMountainArts.com if you would like to join her for a workshop in the mountains.

Image Credits

Poetry and Photography with Friends	Debi Benson Bradford
If You Know Me	Debi Benson Bradford
As the Sun Rises	Debi Benson Bradford
Author Photo	June Davis

All other images: Jeanette Richardson Herring
Overlaid images created with Snapseed.

CPSIA information can be obtained
at www.ICGtesting.com
Printed in the USA
LVHW041112161020
668888LV00004B/151

9 781734 188103